WWJZD: WHAT

First Edition
ISBN-13:978-0-578-54864-7

Publisher: Heade & Hearte LLC.
Ordering Information: Orders by wholesalers: WWJZD:What Would Jay-Z Do? may be purchased in bulk quantities by emailing holla@whatwouldjay-zdo.com. Printed in China.

daily meditations for the culture

quinn
bryant

for my dad.
they don’t make em like you no more.

ride my wave.
to access my curated
WWJZD playlist on **TIDAL**,
subscribe at
whatwouldjay-zdo.com

the author has decided to donate a percentage of the proceeds from the sales of this book to **The Shawn Carter Foundation** help individuals facing socio-economic hardships further their education at post-secondary institutions.

to donate, please go to:
www.shawncartersf.com/donate/

if you've "been praying to god so long that [you're] atheist" and need to be motivated daily by a culture that speaks for you and to you.

may you stay focused, happy and healthy "on the road to riches and diamond rings."

"allow me to reintroduce myself."

public service announcement

the black album

i've always considered myself a JAY-Z fan ... no, thee JAY-Z fan. i used to dream of being on mtv's tv show, fanatic. remember that? probably not. anyway, lyrics? know them. articles? read them. movies? watched them. interviews? studied them. concerts? attended them. hell, i could perform with HOV if m.e.m.p.h.i.s. bleek was for some reason unavailable.

JAY-Z has always been my friend-in-my-head. actually, no, he has been my o.g.-in-my-head. i was introduced to his music in 1996 on a car ride home listening to a late-night Chicago dj after the evening countdown. i'm good. i was about to turn fifteen.

i listened to his lyrics so closely, i probably knew them better than he did. in fact, one time at a show in Chicago at the aragon ballroom, he gave me his bottle of water after he took a couple sips. i like to think that he thought to himself ...
"damn, my mouth is dry. and i know shorty's mouth has gotta be dry 'cause she's been rapping every lyric with me. and singing the chorus. and humming the beat."
true story.

and another one [in my B.I.G. voice]

at another show at Chicago's united center, my oldest friend, evie (my real life tyty), and i came up with a "genius" idea ... we'd make a sign to get his attention.

JAY-Z fans are way too cool to hold up signs at a concert, especially in Chicago. so, we would definitely stand out. we went to work on it. extra thick black permanent markers. hot pink poster board. boom. simple. sweet. to the point. we held it up the entire show while singing along with every. single. lyric. chorus, beat. boom. you're probably thinking ... *'a sign? that's not genius! hell, that's not even original.'* but it was. pretty much. we had the only sign in the sold-out stadium that holds over 20,000 fans.
and our sign didn't generically scream
JAY-Z WE LOVE YOU!
it asked,
TEACH US WHAT YOU KNOW ... PLEASE?
it's the difference between telling a woman you like her body and telling her you like her mind.
the difference between asking someone for food and asking them to teach you how to fish. the difference between a bitch and a sister. the difference between a 4.0 and a 4.6. we knew he'd appreciate that and wouldn't tell us to beat it. guess what? he read it. out loud. on stage. in front of the entire stadium.

"wait, what's that sign say?"
<he mumbles aloud>

can...i get...a... marketing internship?"
<he laughs>
and continues with the run of show. left us standing there, like **wtf? what's our next move?** he was about to end the show and we guessed he would rush to his tour bus and hightail it outta there. so, we rush out to the concourse trying to convince security to let us backstage because JAY-Z had just read our sign. duh. didn't you hear it? no go. a few of them considered it. i'm sure that was the first time they'd had attractive girls asking them to let them backstage so they could get an internship. priceless. they couldn't decide if we were serious or if that was just a well-thought-out con to make ourselves seem more innocent and ambitious than we were. we probably were just another set of groupies. once we'd given up, i was still buzzing' so i run to the payphone to call home and tell my parents the story. this was obviously before everyone had cell phones. there was absolutely no way this could wait until i made it home. my family had clowned us for being so obsessed with JAY-Z. that's just the way my house was. but you could tell they hoped it would work out for us. anyway, before i could get the story out, my stepmom told me she already knew about JAY-Z reading our sign out loud. how? my brother had called. my brother, who couldn't have cared less, had probably used someone

else's change to call home to tell her what happened. he said that JAY-Z had said for the girls with the sign come to the stage.
now, i'm thinking ***"damn, imma be a failure***."
we left too soon. being too eager. now the show was over. like over, over. and we'd spent our time talking to fucking security! ugh.
true story? kinda.
my brother swears to this day that JAY-Z really did come back to the stage and said that. but, i didn't hear it with my own ears so...
"actually, believe half of what you see. none of what you hear, even if it's spat by me."

one last story.
i'll end with this, because this is probably becoming the longest introduction in the history of introductions. i'm sure you wanna get to the point and find out ...
what would jay-z do?
after that encounter at the concert, our engines were revved up like JAY-Z and j.d. in ***money ain't a thang***. but we wondered if we'd ever get that close to our dreams again. what could we do?
obviously, we planned a trip to new york, like we were prince akeem and semi trying to sow our royal oats. looking for the king of New York. we were 20 years old and didn't have a plan at all, but we knew where we needed to be to find the king.
our first trip to the **"concrete jungle where dreams are made of ... there was nothing [we] couldn't do."**

months earlier, on a flight back home to Chicago, evie had befriended a guy that happened to work for roc-a-fella sports. thank you, universe. it was a new subsidiary of roc-a-fella records and this guy was just as eager to share that this was where he worked as we were to learn about what HOV was whipping up in the kitchen. anyway, he was the only person we "knew" in new york, so of course she hit him up. well, he came through, as promised, and brought a friend that happened to get us a step closer to our JAY-Z dreams. this guy is still a good friend of mine to this day. with one sentence he changed the fate of our trip. best. spring break. ever. well, kinda. anyway, we were all talking about new york and he asked us why we liked it so much and all we had for him were references from JAY-Z songs. marcy projects. grey's papaya, etc. he thought we were hysterical, and decided we were harmless and said "did y'all go down to the office?" we look at him like

nigga what? nigga who?

how the hell are we supposed to do that? where the hell is this office? he casually mentions that the address was on the back of the album. duh.

looks like we know what we're doing tomorrow.

boom. so, the next day, we take a train to the office and post up around lunchtime. we figured we could catch a bunch of folks coming in and out in a good mood. we'd found a kinkos and printed up resumes like we had interviews scheduled. we posted up handing out our resumes to whoever would take one telling them that we wanted internships with roc-a-fella. not def jam. roc-a-fella. this wasn't about learning the rap game. this was about learning the crack game. loosely speaking, anyway. we wanted jay-z to teach us what the crack game taught him because, obviously, those lessons and skills were transferable. in life and business. someone finally believed in us or pitied us. either way, it worked in our favor. his name was cadillac tah.

we didn't have a clue who he was, but he seemed super cool and he was giving us an opportunity to shoot our shot. and, he apparently had the juice to make the hating ass security guard that had been giving us the stink eye the whole-time pipe down and give us guest passes. he told her we were with him and he took us up to murder inc's office.

murder inc shared a floor with roc-a-fella. we were right across the hall from jay-z! there were only about two people in the office at the time, but they showed us some love. we told them our story, took pictures and they even offered us an unpaid internship. dope. the guy knew it would be a long shot since we didn't live in new york, but it was on the table if we could make it work. we graciously thanked him and told him we'd be in touch. but for us, it wasn't jay-z. although it would have gotten us across the hall, we decided that murder inc. was cool, but we didn't wanna come work for them and look like traitors once our opportunity presented itself with roc-a-fella. it was coming.

en route to the elevator, guess who gets off the elevator? dame! still not jay-z, but we're getting so fucking close. but damn, dame though? dude was known for being an asshole. but it's now or never. he's in mid-conversation with a group of people. walking quickly. focused. he must've felt us staring at him with

our mouths open because he looks up. i lock eyes with him and start speaking quickly.
mr. dash?
... my resume
... marketing
... internship.
i'm not exactly sure of what the hell i said verbatim, but it went something like that. i think evie was talking at the same time so i couldn't tell which words were mine and which were hers. we scrambled quickly as he extended his hand to accept our resumes without saying a word to us. he didn't seem to miss a beat in the conversation that he was already having. he looked a little confused and mostly unimpressed, but at least he didn't curse us out for interrupting.
still not jay-z, but we were so close. he could've called security on us. lol. evie and i barely speak in the elevator. as we pass the hater security guard on our way out, we both give a cocky smile like ***"who gon stop me, huh?"*** we might have even jumped at her. you couldn't tell us shit! we might as well have just signed a deal.

as soon as we get a safe distance away from the building, we start reliving what had just happened and how close we'd come to JAY-Z. as we stand in the courtyard of the building trying to figure out our next move evie, who has glasses and refuses to wear them squints across the courtyard, casually points and says, *"that looks like tyty."*
"you can't stop i, from drinking mai tais with tyty. down in nevada, haha papa"

now, i, look up. i have amazing vision. well, back then i did. i scream, *"bitch! that's JAY-Z!"*
"oh. my. God. Hov."

how she could have mistaken JAY-Z for tyty, is beyond me. it's like a whole foot height difference between the two. anyway, we take off running in our stacked heels! by this time, JAY-Z is about to climb in the back of the black s.u.v. that is waiting for him on the curb. we're running! the s.u.v. "***pulls off slow***." we're running! the s.u.v. stops at the red light. we just caught a blessing! we run up to the driver's side of the vehicle flashing our resumes with one hand, banging on the window with the other. me at the driver's window. evie is at JAY-Z's heavily tinted window. but we know he can see us. the driver, who is clearly used to this sort of thing, is barely rattled and simply shakes his head no. desperately, we keep banging. resumes plastered against the window because we realize that we don't have much time. the driver cracks the window and says through his caribbean accent... ***"he said take them."*** we quickly shove our resumes in the window smiling showing off every tooth in our mouths. the s.u.v. pulls off.
we just knew JAY-Z would look at the Chicago addresses on our resumes and put 1 and 1 together connecting the dots with our hot pink sign from the Chicago concert months earlier. he and dame had probably just had a conversation about some girls handing him their resumes by the elevator. we fully expected HOV to call us personally to offer us paid in full positions and tell us he has been looking all over for us. we left feeling very satisfied with ourselves. It

was all we could talk about for weeks while we waited by our phones. nothing. just a story to tell. i got us an internship that summer as a result of that story. after months with no response, summer came and went. i now had more beef with JAY-Z than nas,
"fuck JAY-Z." (in my ether voice)
how could he play us like that? we were just trying to get put on some game. we weren't trying to rap, we just wanted to learn.
***"after all the fucking love we showed you,
you want to be a fucking crab?
no more taking up for you,
no more nothing,
you find everything funny,
you wanna take everything as a joke.
fuck you!"***
so, i went from being a fanatic to...i dunno what i became.
i still liked his music. but i didn't want to.
i was pissed!
i went from
"arguing all day about who's the best emcees..."
to only giving people dirty looks if they tried to discount his talent.
i figured it was time to "***come of age, part 2.
hold my own weight. fit my crown."***
years later when i moved to brooklyn, i picked an apartment because it was a block away from marcy projects. right off nostrand ave.

i went to the bathroom once while i was in the 40/40 and he walked past my friends. damn, just missed him. "***you see me stressed, right?***
can i live?"

of course, i'm still a fan of Hov and his movements have only validated what i saw in him from the beginning. i'm proud every time i read about him. i take his wins and lessons personally. some may root for a professional sports team ... but me, i'm rooting for the roc.

i've lived my life in lyrics and i even speak in lyrics. whenever life happens i ask, ***what would JAY-Z do?***

he offers so many jewels. it blows my mind how some songs are loaded with lessons line for line. i didn't know where to start, so i just started writing. you might notice some themes during certain times of year.

fair warning: this book is not my attempt to explain his words, but how i've interpreted the lessons in his lyrics. this is a curated collection of daily meditations based on a fan's life lessons inspired by the lyrics of JAY-Z.

i encourage you to download, stream and continue to revisit JAY-Z's catalog as you incorporate this book into your daily meditations.

january 1
"so, we offer you, well, we offer our lives. what do you bring to the table?"
Can I Live
Reasonable Doubt

everyone wants to eat. but, so often, so many people don't want to cook, go shopping or wash the dishes. that's why potlucks are a good idea. every individual contributes their best for everyone to feast. this is a great representation of teamwork. stop eating with people that aren't contributing their best and won't stick around to clean up the mess. take an assessment of the people you've allowed to have a seat at your table. are their goals aligned with yours? what value are they adding? are they motivating you? supporting you? helping you grow? or are they just taking up a seat and taking food to go?

the food on my table will be in direct proportion to the people at the table.

january 2
"don't be good, my nigga, be great."
F.U.T.W.
Magna Carta ... Holy Grail

sometimes it's easier to be good enough and fly beneath the radar. this way, you don't have to work so hard and you can avoid most criticism. however, you won't get the rewards either!
push yourself to your potential. you've got what it takes to be great. it took over nine months to make you, so you are certainly better than good enough.
you know that feeling when you've come straight from the salon or barbershop? that feeling when you have on a fresh outfit or new shoes. that feeling when you're your goal weight? when your skin is glowing? car is washed. house is clean? when you've checked off everything on your to-do list? live that daily. that's your best self. that's your great. dig deep. do the work that greatness requires. your greatness will make some people uncomfortable but know that it will inspire others. you owe it to yourself to be great. allow your greatness to inspire greatness.

i will show the world the best me.

january 3
"i'd rather die enormous than live dormant."
Can I Live
Reasonable Doubt

i know you've heard the saying, "i'd rather die on my feet than live on my knees." that means you'd rather fight for what you believe in than succumb to someone else's demands and shrink yourself. are you willing to fight to live your best life? stop asking for permission. it's your life. stop worrying about being judged by others. again, it is your life! live loud! make some noise! don't dumb yourself down to make others comfortable. you only have one life, do it big! don't let the days pass you by without splashing around... experience some things. don't think small. don't dim your light. shine bright like the diamond you are.

i will do the world a favor and do me.

january 4
"nobody's built like you, you designed yourself."
A Dream
The Blueprint²: The Gift & The Curse

look around. notice all the different shapes, sizes and shades of the people around you? notice the tones of voice, different hair textures ... even the different smells? now, take another look, and pay attention to the people around you that are dressed in the same style, manipulating their natural hair in the same style just to fit in. do you know what went in to creating you? science did its part, so now it's time for you to do yours. why fit in when you were born to stand out? how else can you explain having siblings with the same mom and dad and not looking and acting exactly alike. you're attracted to different things. you excel in different things. do you. love you. live you. be you.

i am one of one.

january 5
"my ancestors took old food, made soul food."
GHOST OF SOULJA SLIM
A Written Testimony

when life gives you lemons, you make lemonade. i'm sure you've been put in some unimaginable circumstances beyond your control and realized the only thing you can control is how you respond to it. play the hand you're dealt and make the best out of the circumstances you're given. when what you do is done in love, only great things can come. for our ancestors to take someone else's trash and make treasure, with recipes that cannot be duplicated shows you the greatness and resilience that runs through your veins. leave people wondering how the hell you did it. don't let the things that happen to you become you. move forward with the confidence of knowing you ancestors have your back. you've got this and anything else life throws at you. don't be anyone's victim. emerge victorious.

i play my hand.

january 6
"time to separate the pros from the cons."
Brooklyn's Finest
Reasonable Doubt

what is your decision-making process? do you react based on emotion or do you logically strategize and execute your plan? make a list. what are the positives? what are the negatives? do the benefits outweigh the detriments? do the rewards outweigh the risks? does your faith outweigh your fears? be sure to think things through to the end. the best- and worst-case scenarios. that does not mean to overthink. play chess, not checkers. stop reacting to every little thing that has nothing to do with your goal. learn to be more proactive. you should not be making moves that jeopardize your goals. always think big picture and play for the long term.

my risks require calculations.

january 7
"my life is based on sacrifices."
Politics as Usual
Reasonable Doubt

nothing worth having comes easy. set goals for your life and wake up every day and do what you need to do to move closer to those goals. want to lose weight? eat better than you did the day before. wake up earlier and go to the gym. need more money? spend less. sell some things you don't need! cut your costs! do you really need cable with low-cost steaming alternatives? recognize the difference between a want and need and stop buying things you don't need. how many pairs of shoes do you have? how many do you need? are those new shoes necessary? look in your refrigerator. do you have to eat out? listen to your parents' words lingering in your head and remember that there is, in fact, food at home. if you've got some free time, find a part-time job. with rideshare opportunities and air bnb, earning some extra cash is easier than ever. make adjustments to get where you're trying to go. if you are unwilling to make sacrifices, you have to question if you want the things you say you do.

my sacrifices make the reward much sweeter.

january 8
“please, repeat after me. its only one rule... i will not lose.”
Change The Game
The Dynasty: Roc La Familia

it’s up to you whether you win or lose. how hard are you going? how much work are you willing to put in? are you developing your talents? are you doing your research? are you expanding your network? are you building your team? are you collaborating with others? are you allowing yourself to be mentored? winning is a process. there will be ups and downs, ebbs and flows, peaks and values. know when to plan and when to execute. know when to learn and when to teach. set your goal and then pray, plan and execute. the real win is in the learning. no one can take that away from you, but it can always be shared and used to inspire others. what you learn determines whether you’re a sore winner or loser. what you do with it what makes you a winner.

i’m a winner.

january 9
"gotta learn to live with regrets."
Regrets
Reasonable Doubt

lessons generally come dressed up as losses. when you think you've taken a loss you can sometimes spend so much time replaying the situation, thinking about what you could've done differently, that you miss the lesson. sit with the situation and ask yourself what you've learned or should've learned. meditate on it. seek clarity. make sure to take note for the future, so you don't continue to repeat your mistakes. let the experiences of your past make you better, not bitter, and transform those lessons into a know mindset, instead of a no mindset. if you keep reliving your problems of the past, it's because you lack vision for your future.

i will not trip over what's behind me.

january 10
"i will not lose, for even in defeat, there's a valuable lesson learned, so it evens up for me."
Blueprint 2
The Blueprint^2: The Gift & The Curse

losses are just cleverly disguised lessons.
if you're not paying attention, you'll miss countless valuable opportunities to learn and improve yourself. the universe will continue testing you until the lesson is learned. you'll feel like life is challenging you. you may be overwhelmed because you may not understand why. challenges are designed to strengthen you, not break you, so embrace them. remind yourself that you're strong. if you ever feel that your progress has been stalled, take the opportunity to level up.

i will evolve, not repeat.

january 11
“since most of my niggas won't ever work together. you run a check up but they never give you leverage.”
What’s Free
Championships (Meek Mill)

there is a saying that if you want to go fast, go alone, but if you want to go fast, go together. linking with others with the same passion and complimentary skill sets can take your entrepreneurial hopes from the idea phase to reality. or, you could play a significant role in helping build the vision of someone in your network. why not collaborate with your peers instead of being an employee at a company that may not value you, your journey or your culture and limits your potential for growth and ownership. when thinking about your goals, try putting yourself in a collaborative mindset where it suits the situation instead of defaulting to a competitive mindset. your dreams require teams. and sometimes your dream is a component of a larger dream. think of the big picture, make a play and play your position.

i collaborate with like minds to achieve common goals.

january 12
"this game got valleys and peaks."
Can I Live?
Reasonable Doubt

life is full of ups and downs. if you've never been sad, you'd never appreciate happiness. if you were never poor, you'd most certainly take for granted having money. if you were never congested, you'd never appreciate those moments of breathing easy.
when you're at a low point, use that time to train and sharpen your skills to ensure that you're capable of surviving at the top. the lowest lows and highest highs will show you what you're made of and reveal to you your true self. do you give up during the dips or do you get busy? do you coast during the high times or do you flap your wings? life can be a rollercoaster ride, it's up to you to make the best of it at all points.

what goes up, must come down ... but i can always get back up again.

january 13
"all i got is dreams, but nobody else can see. nobody else believes. nobody else but me."
History
More Than A Game

you ever notice how your dreams are so hard to explain once you've awakened? something that felt so real to you only moments earlier makes absolutely no sense to the people you've decided to share them with. you know why? it was your dream! if you've been given a dream, you shouldn't expect others to understand it. that's why it was given to you. for you are the best possible person to bring it to life, despite how unrealistic it may seem or how crazy it may sound to others. dream so big that you can't wait to wake up and make those dreams become reality! i'm sure there was a time when people thought flying was a crazy notion. now, look at us.

my dreams are seeds planted that require water and sunshine.

january 14
"i'm not afraid of dying. i'm afraid of not trying."
Beach Chair
Kingdom Come

fear can be crippling. the fear of failure and fear of death are ranked at the top of the most common things that most people are afraid of. death is life's only guarantee, so there is no point in worrying about it. your worry will not change the outcome. In fact, worrying about it may only bring it more quickly. when it's over, it's over and you won't have to worry about it anymore. fear can sometimes be enough to make people not pursue their dreams, and all they're left with is regrets and thoughts of woulda, coulda, shoulda and what-if. the fear that you feel is not real. it's all in your mind. it's a test to see if you really want what you say you want. if you don't try, you've already failed, so just do it. as we were all taught as children ... if at first you don't succeed, try, try again.

i try my best to do my best.

january 15
"the streets school us to spend our money foolish."
Can I Live
Reasonable Doubt

we tend to wear our wealth on our backs and spend money trying to impress people that we claim to not even like. what are we trying to prove? do you spend money on liabilities instead of assets and investments? do prioritize things that hold absolutely no value? things that if you were ever in a bind you couldn't take them to the bank and cash them? things you can't pass on to your loved ones? foolish things? why are they foolish? think of how long it took you to earn the money to buy those things. how hard did you have to work? what risks did you have to take? don't you want to make things easier for your children? your nieces & nephews? if you could choose to be more responsible with your spending so that your kids will never have to worry about having a roof over their heads even after you're gone, wouldn't you? are you?

i am wise.

january 16
“a wise man told me don’t argue with fools. argue people from a distance can’t tell who is who.”
Takeover
The Blueprint

it’s tempting to engage in arguments, especially when you know you’re right. deciding not to engage requires patience and discipline. in life, people will test you and you will be tempted to respond. don’t. this is a test. i repeat, this is only a test. if you know you’re acting in righteousness, trust that they know that too. there’s no need to try to convince someone of something they already know or that they are refusing to acknowledge. people control their own understanding. not only is it a complete waste of energy, but it also weakens your position. why would a wise man bother to argue with a fool? the foolish person is guaranteed to beat you with their extensive experience in petty arguments and they have succeeded at bringing you down to their level. now you both appear to be fools, and your opponent is much better at it than you are, so they will win every time. don’t give them what they’re asking for.

i won’t abandon my throne to address jokers.

january 17
“they say a midget standing on a giant’s shoulders can see much further than the giant.”
Hovi Baby
The Blueprint²: The Gift & The Curse

learn to use your enemies. as the underdog, there will be certain things that you’re unable to do as effectively as you’d like to alone. you might lack the funding, expertise or muscle that your competitor has. however, they benefit from something you have to offer. learn to use their weakness against them as an opportunity to leverage your strengths. understand where you fit in their mission and leverage that to get where you’re trying to go and gain access to things you might not otherwise have access to.
learn from history. the writings are on the wall. do your research. if you want to be great, do what great people have done. pick up where they left off. learn from and replicate what has already been tried, tested and proven. you don’t have to reinvent the wheel. its already been done. copy, paste, repeat. giants built the pyramids. If hindsight is 20/20, then what are you using history for?

i am forward-thinking.

january 18
"i'm like a dog. i never speak, but i understand."
Never Change
The Blueprint

listening is a lost art. often; people are only waiting to reply instead of listening to understand. this affects the quality of communication drastically. there are things that aren't said that should be observed or felt. there's a reason dogs have earned the title of man's best friend. they don't speak, but they utilize their intuition and pay attention to body language to listen closely. when you're in a bad mood, your dog knows to give you space. when you need to be cheered up, your dog shows you love. when you're speaking your dog offers his undivided attention and responds accordingly. dogs are loyal and protective companions. the reason dogs are all these things is because they are clear on your intentions. how? because of your actions, not your words. you do the things necessary to keep them alive and ensure their safety. how real is that? you make it clear that their life matters. your loyalty to them creates trust and love, without it ever having to be spoken.

i don't discuss what i already understand.

january 19
"what nigga you're broke what the fuck you gon tell me?"
22 Two's
Reasonable Doubt

when you embark on anything and decide to share the news with others, you'll get lots of feedback. you'll receive congratulations, compliments & criticisms. you'll also get lots of unsolicited advice, mostly from people that have never done what you're doing. it's natural to question the validity of that advice. everyone you meet has something to teach you. it's up to you to figure out what that is. sometimes, you must do the opposite of what someone has advised you and other times you have to eat the fish and leave the bones. people are "broke" or "broken" for various reasons. just because someone doesn't know how to save money doesn't mean they don't know how to make it and just because someone can't sing doesn't mean they don't know good music when they hear it. keep an open mind and figure out what you can learn from everyone.

i learn from everyone.

january 20
“they'll cut off the nose to spite their face, they'll steal ya Jesus.”
THE NEVERENDING STORY
A Written Testimony

i’m sure you’ve heard of running off on the plug. what’s that about? once you charge your mobile phone, its only so long that your battery will survive before you have to plug back in. have you ever shared your idea with someone only for them to regurgitate it to you as if you didn’t give the idea in the first place. instead of trying to collaborate with you for something extraordinary, there are people that will completely cut you out, even if it results in a mediocre outcome lacking something essential. if someone provides the fuel for the plane, why would you take off on them because the tank is full. you might be fly for a minute, but trust and believe, that tank will ultimately be on ”e” again. be selective with who you choose to share your ideas, culture and even your food because some are vultures and invaders who are waiting to claim it as their own. chew with your mouth closed.

i protect what’s mine.

january 21
"please, repeat after me. its only one rule... i will not lose."
Change The Game
The Dynasty: Roc La Familia

it's up to you whether you win or lose. how hard are you going? how much work are you willing to put in? are you developing your talents? are you doing your research? are you expanding your network? are you building your team? are you collaborating with others? are you allowing yourself to be mentored? winning is a process. there will be ups and downs, ebbs and flows, peaks and values. know when to plan and when to execute. know when to learn and when to teach. set your goal and then pray, plan and execute. the real win is in the learning. no one can take that away from you, but it can always be shared and used to inspire others. what you learn determines whether you're a sore winner or loser. what you do with it what makes you a winner.

i'm a winner.

january 22
“Hear me clearly: if y'all niggas fear me
Just say y'all fear me
Fuck all these fairy tales
Go to hell; this is God engineering
This is Hail Mary pass; y'all interfering.”
Free Mason
Teflon Don (Rick Ross)

people that hate on you usually aren’t happy with themselves. something about you and your successes makes them think, “why not me?” it makes them question themselves and their ability and instead of leveling up, they make you a target and create imaginary “beefs” with you in their mind, even if they’ve never actually met you. don’t get distracted by the hate. live in your greatness and continue to be who you were created to be. don’t let the hissing of the snakes in the garden take your mind off the birds chirping. keep tending to your garden, planting and watering your seeds and reaping the rewards.

my impact is stronger than the ill feelings of my haters.

january 23
"expectation for dips, for precipitation we stack chips, partly."
Can I Live
Reasonable Doubt

life has its ups and conversely, it has its downs. knowing that, you must be sure to prepare as best as possible for those unavoidable downtimes. learn from camels. if we know there will inevitably be droughts, you should hoard away water when its plentiful in preparation of the times when it is not. don't make the mistake of thinking that the good times will never cease, even temporarily. of course, we'd all love to avoid the bad times, but the bad times show us what we're really made of.

my rainy-day funds make it rain in a drought.

january 24
"everything evens up you just wait, even a garbage can gets a steak."
Guns & Roses
The Blueprint[2]: The Gift & The Curse

the tables eventually turn. it is inevitable. you can be up today, down tomorrow and back up the next day. life is like that. you cannot let the times when you're down get to your heart and you must not let the times when you're up, go to your head. remember that when dealing with others, as well. just because someone is better or worse off than you today, doesn't mean they will stay there. stay humble and stay ready. luck is simply when preparedness meets opportunity. be patient, your time is coming. challenges are meant to test you, not stop you. in moments of difficulty, do not give up, go harder. be consistent in your efforts because something good is coming your way.

i know nothing lasts forever, especially bad times.

january 25
"on the rise to the top, many drop."
Regrets
Reasonable Doubt

when you begin to prioritize your growth and your goals, you'll begin to lose some people that you thought would always be there. don't fret. you'll realize that your "losses" are generally the things that had been preventing your growth and holding you back from reaching the goals that you've set for your life. just how you have to trim your split ends to ensure healthy hair growth, the same thing applies in life. to get where you're going, you'll have to shed: old ways of thinking; old habits; and even old relationships. by shedding your excess baggage, you'll be able to walk through more doors and you'll be able to ascend to further heights. don't be distracted by the things that are falling by the wayside. those things no longer suit your purpose. stay focused on your growth and its role in the pursuit of your goals.

i let go of what's weighing me down so i can fly.

january 26
"how can you fairly assess something from the outside looking in?"
Lucky Me
In My Lifetime Vol. 1

sometimes we judge others without knowing them. we project our biases and assumptions onto others and end up disliking them for things that have nothing to do with them. have you ever hated someone when you first met them and when you finally got a chance to know them, you realized they were pretty cool? have you ever disliked someone because of what someone else told you about them? has someone ever misjudged you unfairly? how many times has someone asked you "what's wrong" and you were just sitting there minding your business, alone with your thoughts? people are fighting battles you have no idea about. the world could use less judgement and more compassion.

i know that some things are gold-plated.

january 27
"i know any type of success breeds envy."
Lucky Me
In My Lifetime Vol. 1

no matter how much good you do or how successful you are, there will be people that are envious of you. love is derived from respect and envy is a form of resentment. in most cases, hate and envy are simply confused admiration of your strength, your power and your impact on others. think about how many people hated dr. martin luther king jr. or those who root against lebron james. as the Basquiat painting points out, most kings get their head cut off. you can't control others' reaction to your success. keep doing you and understand that with love, comes hate. be humbled by the love and encouraged by the hate.

i take the bad with the good.

january 28
"you should just focus on doing what you gotta do because sometimes ... the best way to see a person is not look at them. right? cause if you're looking at them, they gonna [you know] be on their best behavior."
Money Goes, Honey Stay
Loso's Way (Fabolous)

stay focused, man. relationships, friendships and family can sometimes be a distraction from your goals. people pretend well and are not always who you think they are or who they profess to be. remember that people can only pretend for so long. so, if you're focusing on doing you, you won't have much time to be focusing on their moves. let them do what they want to do, so you can see what they'd rather do. time will reveal whether a person is holding you down or trying to hold you up. don't slow up your progression by focusing on the wrong people.

i'm focused on the right things.

january 29
"if you're balling, keep balling. if you're jealous, stop."
Real Niggaz
In My Lifetime Vol. 1

jealousy is a useless trait. it has absolutely no value. in fact, it just makes you a hater. what you say about others says more about you than it does about them. be honest with yourself in moments when you may find yourself spreading hate. there's enough good to go around and we all have the same twenty-four hours to work towards our goals. so, get to it.

"what? ain't no more to it." – notorious b.i.g.

i don't have time for hating, because i'm grinding.

january 30
"don't even hate on those who hate me."
Can I Live II
Reasonable Doubt

people will hate you because you being you makes them feel a way about themselves that they don't quite understand. we're quick to respond to that hate with more hate. you may hate someone because they're confident and your low self-esteem causes you to interpret it as arrogance. you may hate someone because they're attractive and you interpret it as narcissism. hating someone or hating on someone consumes too much of your energy. energy that could be spent building yourself up. don't waste precious time hating on someone that you could be learning from. let that bad energy go. greet people with love and good intentions and those with good intentions will reciprocate. this will make the people with bad intentions easier to identify.

i cure hate with love.

january 31
"nobody wins when the family feuds."
Family Feud
4:44

family are people placed in your life by god. your family is intended to offer you a glimpse of the people you will meet in life. some good, some bad. the challenge you're presented with is to love them unconditionally, despite their flaws. just because you love someone, does not necessarily mean that you will like them. your familial relationship will give you insight as to what factors cultivated the person before you ... good and bad. it is not meant for you to judge, but to offer perspective. that perspective should help you understand how to engage with them to help make your family stronger. we are all apart of various families. first your immediate family, then your mom's family, your dad's family, your neighborhood, your city, etc. think about the family feud game show, notice how those families work together to win over the other, regardless of what differences they may have.

i work collaboratively to get the win.

february 1
"we know the pain is real, but you can't heal what you never reveal."
Kill Jay Z
4:44

life happens. things will happen to you, both good and bad. do you broadcast the good and bury the bad? realize that all these things, good and bad, make you who you are. they affect your perspective. they affect your relationships, both with yourself and with others. they affect the decisions you make for your life. these things make your life more colorful. the good things make your life pretty. the bad things make your life more interesting. according to Rumi, the wound is the place where the light enters you. don't let heartbreak and heartache harden your heart but allow it to open it. write in a journal or find a professional therapist that you're comfortable with to lighten the things that have been weighing you down. only then can you grow with a freedom you've never felt. we all have our shit and all shit stinks. take a look at it before you flush the memory of it and move forward with relief.

i confront my problems.

february 2
"i break bread with the late heads. picking they brains for angles and all the evils that the game will do."
D'evils
Reasonable Doubt

there is a lot to be learned from our elders. you've got to know where you come from to know where we're going. there is nothing new under the sun. history repeats itself, there are just new characters. so, everything that happens is just a reinvention of something that has already been. being armed with history's lessons from those that have lived it, in addition to the lessons that they've learned from those before them, can be a tremendous benefit. listening to elders' stories about their successes and failures and learning from them can save you time, money and heartbreak.

i learn from the mistakes of others.

february 3
"please, repeat after me. its only one rule... i will not lose."
Change The Game
The Dynasty: Roc La Familia

it's up to you whether you win or lose. how hard are you going? how much work are you willing to put in? are you developing your talents? are you doing your research? are you expanding your network? are you building your team? are you collaborating with others? are you allowing yourself to be mentored? winning is a process. there will be ups and downs, ebbs and flows, peaks and values. know when to plan and when to execute. know when to learn and when to teach. set your goal and then pray, plan and execute. the real win is in the learning. no one can take that away from you, but it can always be shared and used to inspire others. what you learn determines whether you're a sore winner or loser. what you do with it what makes you a winner.

i'm a winner.

february 4
"the percentage who don't understand is higher than the percentage who do."
Can I Live II
Reasonable Doubt

don't get frustrated when people aren't aligned with your way of thinking or your position of truth. most people follow the established beliefs of the masses and regurgitate miseducation, despite having evidence to the contrary. critical thinking is not so common, and a minority of people independently form opinions based on research, logic and reason. what about you? people won't likely understand your assessments that differ for the norm and they will criticize your thinking outside of the box and going against the grain. in fact, they will condemn your determination that there is no box. you must be willing to understand peoples' thinking and move forward in your truth. find your people, the ones that get it, and exchange ideas and information amongst like minds. smile and nod with everyone else.

i understand.

february 5
"to all my brothers it ain't too late to come together."
22 Two's
Reasonable Doubt

there is a saying that if you want to go quickly, go alone and if you want to go far, go together. do you work well with others? so often we break apart from the group, ignoring the benefits of unification and find ourselves feeling isolated and guarded and ultimately fighting with the people we should be building with. we're stronger in numbers, just look at your hand when is balled into a fist. what do you think would have more impact... one person doing the electric slide or one thousand? get in formation. we do not have to agree on every little point, we just have to want the same outcome. you can't fight a war amongst yourselves. don't get caught up on the people that aren't joining. they'll either catch up or take their own path. life is hard enough and isolation is dangerous.

i know that two heads are better than one.

february 6
"even if it ain't sunny, hey i ain't complaining."
Feelin' It
Reasonable Doubt

sunny days are the best. they provide energy and motivation to get things done. the warmth of the sun provides comfort, and the light of the sun can feel like a spotlight, and you are the superstar. sunny days offer you a fresh perspective and put a filter on your life that seems to wash away the blemishes that cloudy days seem to amplify. these days can, sometimes cause you to succumb to the bad energy and focus your attention on the things that are going wrong instead of being grateful for all the many blessings in your life, including the fact that you're alive. just consider all the people that didn't have an opportunity to see the new day. don't sweat the small stuff and remain in a state of gratitude. remember that every day above ground is a good day and without the rain, the crops would not grow.

i smile because i'm alive and i've got options.

february 7
"start a society, within society."
Legacy
4:44

don't sit around complaining about the things in the world that you detest. align with people that share your frustrations and work towards solutions. connect with like minds and similar values and who's aspirations for life and what the world mirror yours. work together to be the change you wish to see in the world and manifest that change through your choices and actions in how you live your life every single day.

i will be the change i want to see.

february 8
"it's room on the bandwagon don't abort."
Marcy Me
4:44

generally hopping on the bandwagon can be perceived negatively. but in order to be an effective leader, you have to have followers. these days everyone wants to be the chief, with no indians. followers should believe in the mission and values as the leader and believe in their ability to lead. martin had followers and so did Malcolm. without those followers they wouldn't have been able to make to monumental impact that allowed them to solidify their places in history and illicit change. it's nothing wrong with following when the goal is to push to culture forward and improve the lives of the people. as long as you know who you're following and what they stand for, don't let the judgment of others prevent you from following a good cause. if you're coming, come on.

i play my position.

february 9
"partner, i'm still spending money from '88."
Dead Presidents
Reasonable Doubt

when did you make the money you're spending now? two hours ago? two weeks ago? a month? a year? ten years? how liberating can that be to not have a "if you don't work you don't eat" mentality? to not live paycheck to paycheck. to not have your money spent before it has been earned. how dope would that be to know that the paycheck you earned today ensures that the kids you haven't even conceived yet have a safe place to live? attend the best schools. see the world. how much stress would that relieve from your shoulders only to be replaced with motivation. having this type of financial cushion provides a level of confidence and freedom to explore investment opportunities and learnings that constantly having to react to your financial needs does not. ask yourself, "what year am i spending money from?'

i earn for future generations.

february 10
"generational wealth that's the key."
Marcy Me
4:44

how much money do you earn? how much money have you saved? how much money are you investing? how much money are you spending? do you spend so much money that you're left broke before you even cash your paycheck? how much of the money you're spending is on things your children can inherit? they can't do anything with those expensive dinners, car payments, or that apartment. be clear about who you're doing that for. are you making moves to give your children the head start that you wish you'd had? how much better would you be doing if you'd inherited a house to live in? rental property? money to start the business you've been dreaming about. if you didn't have student loans? if your family owned a business for you to work in or expand on?

i won't buy my children the things i wanted, i will teach them what I needed to know.

february 11
"""y'all be chasing. i replaced em."
I Just Wanna Love U (Give It 2 Me)
The Dynasty: Roc La Familia

don't ever beg anyone to be in your life. if they can't see what's amazing about you, then that's on them. if you can't see what's amazing about you, then that's on you.
you should not have to convince anyone that you're dope ... if that's what you're doing, you may be the one that needs convincing. it's okay to be confused as to why some folks can see it, but remember, some people are blind ... and others just have different palates. your brand of dope might not suit their taste ... and that is okay. the non-negotiable requirement for someone taking a spot in your life should be that they fuck with you ... the long way. otherwise, you need to ask yourself, why you even think they're worthy of the time you have. get over them and get on with your life.

i move on to the next.

february 12
"i can't wait to give this shit to my children."
4:44
4:44

everyone wants to give their kids the things they never had. are you thinking big picture? or are you just thinking about the shoes you wanted that your mama couldn't buy you? if so, you missed the whole point. don't focus on the shoes, focus on why your mom couldn't buy them. who gets rich from those things? not you! did you like getting hand me downs growing up? no, because those hand-me-downs were worthless and out of style. but imagine being handed a house? a rental property that provides monthly income? a lump sum of money to invest? a collection of valuable artwork? classic cars or timepieces? you'd appreciate and understand the sacrifices your parents made a lot more, wouldn't you? not only would your parents have equipped you with lessons about saving, investing and what's important, you'd understand that the work you do is most rewarding when it continues to pay your family for generations.

my wealth will better the lives of my children's children.

february 13
"nothing's impossible."
Jay-Z & Dean Baquet Interview
The New York Times Style Magazine
September 29, 2017

your only limitations are in your mind and you don't give yourself enough credit. have some faith in yourself and have faith that the most high has equipped you with everything you require to become everything that you are meant to be. everything seems impossible at first, until it's done. then you wonder why it took you so long to do it. don't let your self-imposed fears and lack of self-confidence interfere with you accomplishing your goals. be crazy enough to believe in yourself and your ability to get things done, make things happen and turn your wildest dreams into your reality. live your dreams, don't squander the opportunities that life provides you.

i'm possible.

february 14
"either love me or leave me alone."
Public Service Announcement
The Black Album

people will sometimes enter your life and profess to love you but somehow, it'll feel like the exact opposite. some will spend all your time together tearing you down, others may constantly be trying to change you. understand that this is not about you, but it is about them. they may not know what love is or the way that they show love may not be aligned with how you receive love. love should bring out the best in you and help you grow. love should help you become a better version of yourself and encourage you to reciprocate that love. love is a verb. you have to actively show it. not just holidays or special occasions, but every day. be good to the people you love and make sure that the people you love are being good to you. you have to love yourself enough to separate yourself from anything that does not feel like love. love builds you up, and if you are frowning more than you're smiling, understand that that is not love.

love operates in my best interest.

february 15
"friend or foe, yo? state your biz."
Friend or Foe
Reasonable Doubt

a friend is a person in which you have a mutual affection for, and they offer support. a foe is the exact opposite. if you don't like someone or if you have no interest in supporting them, don't refer to them as your friend, because now that makes you a snake. stop calling people your friends because it sounds good. friendship creates expectations and assuming a title and posing as a friend without meeting those expectations creates the assumption that your intentions were to deceive. be clear about your relationships and meet those expectations. show love to your friends. support your friends. assume that your friends have positive intentions and make sure yours are the same.

i am friendly to my friends.

february 16
"man, you was who you was 'fore you got here"
Public Service Announcement (Interlude)
The Black Album

you were born with all the potential in the world. your environment can nurture or hinder that potential. it will either bring out the best in you or the worst. whether it does the former or latter is 100% up to you and your mindset. are you determined to win, or will you give in? will you sink or swim? life is about the survival of the fittest, and you've already survived the first challenge ... you were conceived. of the millions of sperm released, you are a result of those that survived fertilize the egg. you are the result of the strength of your those that came before you. don't you ever forget it.

i'm a survivor.

february 17
"we must not let outsiders violate our blocks."
Hard Knock Life
Vol. 2 ... Hard Knock Life

protect what's yours. your neighborhood. your family. your friends. your relationships. your goals. your plans. your dreams. your health. your life. align with others that want the same safety, security and prosperity and form a community. stop letting others disrupt your peace. don't let homewreckers wreck your relationship. don't let unfriendly people infiltrate your friendships. don't let people that don't value family join your yours. we're only as strong as our weakest link, so the actions of those amongst you reflects on and influences you. make sure everyone in your community is doing what is best for the community as a whole, not only what's best for them but to the detriment of the greater good.

i protect my peace.

february 18
"to make a nigga die bleeding is nothing. you make a muthafucka die breathing then you're saying something."
You're Only A Customer
Streets Is Watching

generally, when someone feels that they've been wronged or disrespected and they've failed to resolve the issue through communication they default to violence, and in some cases even something final. that's major. especially for an offense that in the grand scheme of life may be relatively minor. it is true that success is the best revenge. imagine a person that's been hating on you being forced to see you win every single day. imagine someone that has shown you disrespected you, be ignored by you and those that respect you. that'll teach them. don't make irrelevant people feel relevant by responding to them. if they can't beat you, they'll have no other choice than to try to join you, leaving you to hold the cards and the power.

i won't throw rocks at every dog that barks along my journey.

february 19
"whatever jigga say, jigga probably do."
Streets Is Talking
The Dynasty: Roc La Familia

are you intentional with your actions? or do you just fly by the seat of your pants? are you thoughtful with your words? or do you just like to hear yourself talk? if someone fact checked the things you said, would you be validated or voided. don't just talk because you have lips. make sure what you're saying is actual and factual. make sure you're informed of what you're speaking about. add value to the conversation. not uniformed opinions, unfounded judgements and fruitless dreams. don't just talk about it, be about it.

my word is my bond.

february 20
“why throw everything away over ego?”
Trouble
Kingdom Come

you’ve got shit to do. period. if you don’t, you’re probably one of the people fucking with the people that actually have shit to do trying to get them off their square. but, for those of you with dreams, goals, plans, people to make proud ... even if it’s just making yourself proud ... stay focused. distractions are intended to test you. hits to your ego are opportunities to practice being humble. success is sweeter when you’re humble. so, when someone or something tests you and you’re tempted to react in a manner that puts your vision for your future at risk, take a moment to consider what’s most important to you. if your ego wins, your goals aren’t big enough, so think bigger.

i’m keeping both eyes on the prize.

february 21
"most bullies, bully."
Jay-Z & Dean Baquet Interview
The New York Times Style Magazine
September 29, 2017

bullies come in all shapes, sizes, and ages. they also manifest in different areas of your life whether it be family, friends, or work. your bully might be your mom, your boss, your wife, a social media follower or your best friend.

a bully's goal is to intimidate and to force you to cower in their presence, so they appear stronger, more confident or more important than they actually are. if you give in, they win. if you encourage someone bullying another person, they win, and they've also brought you down to their level. don't be surprised or amused by the actions of bullies. they're living up to their title. bullies usually back down when you stand up for yourself.

i am not a victim. i am a hero.

february 22
"i'm not looking at you dudes, i'm looking past you."
Heart Of The City (Ain't No Love)
The Blueprint

the only person you should be in competition with is yourself. look in the mirror, are you better than you were yesterday? are you consistently advancing towards the specific, measurable, attainable, realistic goals that you've set for yourself? it can be helpful to be aware of other's achievements and to do a quick competitive analysis of others in your industry but, if you spend too much time looking in someone else's direction you might trip. keep your eyes on your own paper! the goal is ahead of you, stay focused. don't allow yourself to be distracted by what others are doing. sometimes, paying attention to what others are doing gives both you and them a distorted perspective of their role in your story.

i am not distracted by what others are doing.

february 23
“nobody would fall, cause everyone would be each other’s crutches.”
Feelin’ It
Reasonable Doubt

crutches were designed to help people move forward despite having suffered temporary or permanent setbacks. people have the ability to be that for each other. life consists of ups and downs. setups and setbacks. just because you’re down at the moment, doesn’t mean you will always be. these are the times that it is beneficial to have a network that is willing to lift you up in an effort to maintain your progress and return you to your spot at the top. you also must be willing to reciprocate and do that for others in their time of need. We are only as strong as our weakest link. there is no promise in being the only talent on the team.

i uplift others.

february 24
"my life is getting too wild, i need to bring some sort of calm to it. bout to lose it. voices screaming 'don't do it!'"
This Can't Be Life
The Dynasty: Roc La Familia

arguments with family? trouble at school or work? beefing with friends and foes? road rage? fights in the club? are you all about the drama, but always consider yourself the victim? knock it off! take control of your life if things just keep spiraling. what could you be doing differently? where are you hanging? who are you hanging with? what are you doing? how are you responding? when are you going to change? why are you attracted to or attracting drama? figure your shit out and stop running towards fires and crying when you get burned. work on getting some peace of mind instead of functioning in chaos. breathe. think about what you're doing before you do it and how you're reacting before you respond. you control you. so, do what you need to do.

i am at peace in my environment.

february 25
"lock my body, can't trap my mind."
Can I Live
Reasonable Doubt

being enslaved or incarcerated takes away your physical freedom. it has the power to control what and when you're able to eat, when you can play, etc. it doesn't have the power to control your free thought if you don't allow it to do so. how strong are you mentally? how do you spend your time? educating yourself and reading? you must be selective about what you consume. a mind stretched by new information and experiences will never return to its old dimensions. despite being incarcerated, detroit red evolved to Malcom X, as a result of the people he began to surround himself, the food he chose to consume and with the information he consumed. don't fall into the trap.

i won't allow my growth to be stunted.

february 26
"now the nets a stone throw from where i used to throw bricks. so, it's only right i'm still tossing 'round knicks."
Seen It All (Feat. JAY Z)
Seen It All: The Autobiography (Jeezy)

why is the goal to move out of the hood instead of planting and watering seeds to create a safe, beautiful, flourishing community? you can literally invest in your community to develop a place that you and others would like to live in so no kid will ever again have to hope to get out of the hood. add some value to the place and the people that raised you. be a role model for the kids growing up after you. show them something different. redefine what success is to them. don't succumb to and complain about what's wrong with your neighborhood, be the one change it.

i put on for my city.

february 27
“too much black and too much love equals forever.”
22 Two’s
Reasonable Doubt

Malcolm X once said, “if you're not careful, the newspapers will have you hating the people who are being oppressed and loving the people who are doing the oppressing.” sometimes, out of frustration we can become hateful towards those closest to us that are also frustrated at their circumstances. hate begets more hate, which ultimately erupts into violence. loving others requires courage. love cultivates strength and creates a special bond that comes from wanting the best for another person. love suggests a genuine interest in wanting to see another person happy, healthy and progressing. how could you not thrive in an environment of love? it’s never too late to move beyond the trauma of the past and give love a try.

i believe in the power of love.

february 28
"i seen niggas before me, with a chance to write they own script, slip up and change the story."
Streets Is Talking
The Dynasty: Roc La Familia

this life is yours and yours alone. you get to write the story. although you can't control every single detail, you get to decide most of the aspects. who are the characters? are they extras or do they have a major supporting role? are they encouraging you to do dope shit or are they influencing you to do bullshit? what's the setting? the city? the neighborhood? the wardrobe? are you in pursuit of happiness? success? health? or are you just letting life happen to you? make the days count. first write down the ideal outcome to your story, then get busy living each chapter. don't allow yourself to be distracted by the things and people that don't support your vision. invest your time, money and attention into developing your own story.

i am the author of my life.

february 29
"to live life, get your shit right & play. don't get it twisted like braids, if i miss that's ok. but life's short don't miss a day."
If I Should Die
Vol. 2 ... Hard Knock Life

the only thing we a guaranteed in life is death. we are not guaranteed any amount of time. the problem is that you think you have time. somehow, we move about without intention as if we don't have a limited amount of time on earth. how many times have you postponed something on your to-do list or bucket list until the next day? are you truly taking advantage of the time you have? are you sharpening your skills? are you shooting your shot? are you living in the moment and being present or are you distracted by your vices and devices? are you looking at your phone instead of the person in front of you? are you reminiscing about the past or anxious about the future? how many opportunities, experiences and precious moments are you missing because of your refusal to seize the day and live in the moment?

i am present and will seize the day.

march 1
"my life is getting too wild, i need to bring some sort of calm to it. bout to lose it. voices screaming 'don't do it!'"
This Can't Be Life
The Dynasty: Roc La Familia

arguments with family? trouble at school or work? beefing with friends and foes? road rage? fights in the club? are you all about the drama, but always consider yourself the victim? knock it off! take control of your life if things just keep spiraling. what could you be doing differently? where are you hanging? who are you hanging with? what are you doing? how are you responding? when are you going to change? why are you attracted to or attracting drama? figure your shit out and stop running towards fires and crying when you get burned. work on getting some peace of mind instead of functioning in chaos. breathe. think about what you're doing before you do it and how you're reacting before you respond. you control you. so, do what you need to do.

i am at peace in my environment.

march 2
“it gets tedious, so I keep one eye open like cbs.”
Can I Live
Reasonable Doubt

be aware of your surroundings and who you’re surrounded by. i always find it interesting when people behave in a manner that’s untrustworthy to people that they sleep with. you’re most vulnerable when you’re asleep as both eyes are closed, and you even have a period where. you are literally putting your life in the hands of the person that you’re sleeping with and entrusting them with your most precious gift night after night. this action indicates the utmost trust. who are you allowing to make your food? drive you around? pour and watch your drinks? do you trust the people around you enough to put your life in their hands? what have they done that makes them worthy of your trust? people should not be given your trust by default. stay alert and stay woke. don’t let your guard down because someone professes to be trustworthy. you have got to look out for your wellbeing first.

i’m awake and aware.

march 3
"you was right, niggas want you to be miserable with them."
Regrets
Reasonable Doubt

have you ever had someone close to you be jealous of your happiness or success? if so, what was the state of their life? were they happy? were their affairs in shambles? did they expect you to go beyond being supportive and literally go through the trenches with them and be just as sad at their misfortunes as they are, regardless of whether it directly affects you? there is a difference between sympathy and empathy. it is unreasonable for anyone to demand your suffering to validate that you are sympathetic to theirs. there is a difference between being supportive and being a fool. the people you're surrounded by should lift you up, not pull you down. when you're sad, do you want others to be sad too? check yourself, then check your surroundings.

i will not keep misery company.

march 4
"let your shit bubble quietly."
Coming Of Age
Reasonable Doubt

work hard in silence, let your success make the noise for you. i call that working smart. you waste valuable time and energy running your mouth about what you're doing instead of just doing it. also, boasting makes you a target. it also creates an opportunity for others to form unmanageable expectations of you and you don't want to over-promise and underdeliver. your big plans, big moves and big words can also cause others to be envious of you and that envy manifests as hate, negative talk and negative energy that can hover like a dark cloud over your dreams. don't invite negativity with your big mouth. don't talk yourself out of your blessings. imagine how sweet the reward is when you surprise everyone with your success.

i let my silent success kills loud haters.

march 5
"let them other niggas get the name, skip the fame. 10 thou or a hundred g keep your shit the same."
Coming Of Age
Reasonable Doubt

fame and popularity can distract you from what's important. while its enticing to be a celebrity (locally, regionally, nationally, or globally), consider if that celebrity adds value to you or if it merely boosts your ego. no one likes a show-off and there is no need to make announcements about what you have. understand that while all the fans are watching you, so are the streets and that unwanted attention can bring some unwanted occurrences. jealousy and envy are very real and can fuel some heinous actions. be reminded that as quickly as your blessing are received, they can easily be taken away. stay humble and grateful.

i am humble and focused.

march 6
“we're all trying to win, but then again, maybe it's for the best though, 'cause when they're seeing too much, you know they're trying to get you touched.”
D’evils
Reasonable Doubt

full transparency is rare and should be reserved only for those that will only leave your life in death. only those that view your wins as their own. only those people that are genuinely supporting your efforts to win and whose goals are connected to yours. even then, you may get it wrong sometimes and the wrong people knowing too much of your business may potentially eventually view you as a threat and perceive your gains as their losses. take an assessment of the people in your life. the people that you share your dreams and successes with should have a place in those dreams and successes. if you can recall some side eyes, dry claps and shade, reconsider why they’re on your team.

i make sure everyone in my boat is rowing and not poking holes.

march 7
"hoes'll get you sidetracked and clapped at close feet."
Can I Live
Reasonable Doubt

all relationships demand that you commit some of your time. the goal is to have relationships with those whose direction is aligned with yours. this way they'll contribute to keeping you focused instead of becoming a distraction. do you want the same lifestyle? do you both understand the sacrifices required? if you want to work out every morning but your girlfriend wants to cuddle in bed, this may pose a problem. if you want to go to church each week but your husband is an atheist, this may cause a different issue. if you want to follow a vegetarian diet but your wife's recipes all include meat, what then? what happens when you want to travel the world, but your friends are local? how can you stay focused on saving money if you keep allowing yourself to be persuaded to go out every night? how bad do you want the things that you say you want? enough to change your circle to encouragers and eliminate distractions and disruptions? the choice is yours.

i will not be distracted.

march 8
“too many ladies give these niggas too many chances, too many brothers wanna be lovers don’t know what romance is.”
22 Two’s
Reasonable Doubt

you teach people how to treat you by what you allow. sometimes we get caught up in interpreting a person’s actions, looking at a person’s potential or choosing to nag in the hopes of change when someone doesn’t meet our expectations. when you were a child, what was the most effective means of correction that your parents could administer? a talking to or withholding the things you want? how many times have you given someone numerous chances to treat you right and they eventually got it right? but when you leave, the person recognizes the error of their ways. that’s why so many men get it right with the next woman. you didn’t break him in, you taught him a lesson. why stick around for bad behavior that doesn’t make you feel good? you don’t get what you deserve, you get what you allow. be clear and be realistic about your expectations and stick to them. if you don’t take yourself seriously, why should anyone else?

i know when to move on.

march 9
"too many bitches stuck up from too many sexual advances."
22 Two's
Reasonable Doubt

don't get caught in your own hype. outer beauty eventually fades. accept compliments from suitors as reminders of the physical gifts that God has bestowed on all his creations. you have very little to do with your outer beauty, it is an act of God, so compliments are in recognition of your creator. it's those compliments starting in your youth that help develop your self-confidence, don't let it become arrogance. don't let those compliments about your outward appearance turn you ugly on the inside. your inward appearance is totally up to you and this is really your opportunity to shine and show the world exactly how beautiful you really are.

i carry myself with grace.

march 10
"without people, being rich would be very boring."
Jay-Z & Dean Baquet
The New York Times Style Magazine
September 29, 2017

lots of people think money would solve all their problems. are you one of them? while money might solve a lot of the financial challenges you are dealing with, it definitely won't solve all your problems. some things may change, including you. will you give in to the evils that sometimes accompany acquiring wealth or will you give back? having money makes you who you really are, and it won't make your fans, friends, family or significant others genuinely likely you. they certainly may act like it to your face. people will tolerate you only if you're of benefit to them. would you be willing to give up all the people that genuinely have your back for a chance at being rich? good lives consist of good people. there's absolutely nothing wrong with making money, but don't let money make you.

i value my relationships more than money.

march 11
"even a broken clock is right at least two times a day."
Guns & Roses
The Blueprint[2]: The Gift & The Curse

there may be periods of time where you feel as if you can't do anything right and the whole world is closing in on you. have faith that this will not always be the case. don't let temporary failures get to your head or your heart. stop doubting yourself. stick with it, stay focused, and stay motivated. keep up the pace and keep working and re-working and improving until you finally get things right. your time will come, just be ready. you won't always be wrong, nor will you always right. just keep swinging.

i expect that things will go right for me.

march 12
"I stay on my grind, never stop for bitches."
Stick 2 The Script
The Dynasty: Roc La Familia

it's easy to get distracted from your goals. there are lots of shiny things on the sidelines that can take your eyes off the road to success and riches. keep your eyes on the road. work while others spend. study while others party. keep planting seeds while others prematurely celebrate. anyone that's with you should be grinding too, not distracting you from your grind. make sure you're thinking long-term and surrounding yourself with individuals that are contributing to your grind instead of distracting you from it or undeservedly reaping the rewards. play later and exercise discipline. don't allow short term rewards distract you from long term gains.

i am focused.

march 13
“she knows my purpose wasn't purpose. i ain't perfect, i care.”
December 4th
The Black Album

our mothers have sacrificed so much for us, starting with their bodies. they literally shared their bodies with us to allow us a safe place to grow. they raise us and care for us before we are even able to communicate with words. hell, they teach us to speak. as a result, our mothers usually know us better than anyone. they recognize our potential before we do because they've played a tremendous role in cultivating it. they've instilled morals and values in us, to help guide us, that cannot be erased, although they may sometimes be temporarily forgotten. When you become a parent, you too will take on the role of being your child's first teacher, biggest fan, therapist and biggest motivator. get it right and give them the tools, support and experiences they require to be great. just because you may occasionally get off track, remember that you have a purpose bigger than your missteps.

my purpose is a life of purpose.

march 14
"invisible ink, i had to read things that wasn't there. memories may sneak down my cheek, but i could see a side-eye in my sleep."
Caught Their Eyes
4:44

pay attention to body language. it sometimes speaks louder than words. notice when conversations get dry when you have good news. pay attention to patterns and be think about if you didn't call how long would it take a person to reach out to you? possibly never again. be clear that those are not your people. don't fuss, don't fight, don't argue. just fall back. understand that their mission in your life was to help you discern who is for you and who is not and to learn to let go even when you may have had some fun times in the past. surround yourself with those that value your presence, encourage your success, root for your rise or do they kick you when you're down. are they tolerating you or do they view you as a blessing? use your intuition, to help you get in tune.

i allow energy to guide me.

march 15
“my homey strick told me, "dude finish your breakfast."
Public Service Announcement (Interlude)
The Black Album

do you go to the movies and decide halfway through that it’s too long and walk out of the theatre? what if your favorite athletes decided at half time that the game was too challenging and quit? it’s easy to come up with an idea and kick it off, but it’s your follow-through that really shows what you’re made of. ideas come a dime a dozen, but it’s the execution of those ideas that separate the real from the fake, the hobbies from your passion. finish things with the same momentum that you started them with. start strong, finisher stronger.

i finish what i start.

march 16
"shake hands, make friends like it's all innocent."
1-900-Hustler
The Dynasty: Roc La Familia

never outshine the master. the phrase "no new friends" has become so popular that folks are missing valuable opportunities to network. opportunities to connect with others on similar paths that may help them further their agenda. just because someone isn't your friend, doesn't mean they're your enemy. they might be an ally. don't get so caught up in trendy taglines of those that have already fulfilled their dreams, that you overlook chances that you're given, or people placed in your life to help you fulfill yours. don't be a user and take advantage of people, leverage opportunities to advance.

i am as strong as my network.

march 17
"take your time when you're liking a guy. cause if he sense that your feelings too intense, its pimp or die."
Soon You'll Understand
The Dynasty: Roc La Familia

the beginning of a relationship is usually the best. that's when both of you are being your best selves ... your representative. those butterflies in your stomach can fly away with your common sense. chew your food. taste it. enjoy it. taste the ingredients. you may find there's something that you don't like so much. don't just keep shoveling it down your throat because it tastes good. how many times have you met someone that you liked and gave it all away upfront only for the relationship, that you thought had potential, to crash and burn. when you looked back on it, i'm sure you noticed some things that you could've done differently. for instance, taking your time to get to know who a person really is. not, who you want them to be.

march 18
"if i can't live by my word, then i'd much rather die."
Thank You
The Blueprint 3

never promise what you cannot produce. you are what you do, not what you say you'll do. Even though your intentions might be good, your actions are better. when you don't keep your word, you lose credibility in the eyes of those that you want to earn the trust of, regardless of what your intentions are. be honest with yourself and others about what you can realistically do. don't make promises that you can keep. when you have good intentions, you make promises, but when you have good character, you keep those promises.

my word is my bond.

march 19
"this fuck everybody attitude ain't natural."
Kill Jay-Z
4:44

it's okay to be in your feelings sometimes. you're human. life happens and it's tempting to want to withdraw. keep in mind that you're not always the victim, sometimes you're the one causing hurt and pain to others. hurt people, hurt people. it's usually not personal. people sometimes fight their own demons through other people. try respond to the hurt with love, even if it's from a distance. if you allow yourself to harden and put up a wall to keep the wrong people out, you also are preventing the right people from getting in and getting to know the awesome person that is you. you're preventing people from loving you. love is vital. if you're not feeling anything then you're numb. if you're numb you can neither feel love nor harm, and love feels so good. i wouldn't trade that feeling for anything. would you?

i love others because they are reflections of me.

march 20
“you got a knot in your chest, imagine how a knife hurt.”
Kill Jay-Z
4:44

we are all dealing with things internally. these things can sometimes cause us to lash out at others in various ways, physically and verbally, when we feel that we’ve been wronged in some way. other times, we internalize our stress, and it results in anxiety and panic attacks. if you’ve ever had an anxiety attack, you know the heaviness associated with it and how it can even impact you physically. if your own stress can hurt you imagine how your outward reactions to that stress can hurt others. work on healing the things that cause you anxiety and find healthy ways to manage and respond to stressful situations. by doing this, you can avoid explosive reactions.

i will heal myself so i don’t hurt others.

march 21
"unless you was me, how could you judge me?"
Renegade
The Blueprint

have you ever been encouraged to be yourself and then been judged for it? don't worry. those people are committed to misunderstanding you because you're not who they want you to be. only you and your god know your heart and your story. it is your thoughts about yourself that matter most, but don't be too hard on yourself. you know when you're not living up to your potential and you also know when you're being your best self. get in tune and make adjustments. don't let the praise of others go to your head and don't let others' judgments get to your heart. you were created to be real, not perfect. besides, who determines what is considered perfect? life is about making mistakes, reflecting, learning and improving so that you can become a better version of yourself. there are no ideally perfect people, and the creator is the only one capable of accurately assessing his creations.

only god can judge me.

march 22
"if it wasn't for these pictures, they wouldn't see me at all."
Oceans
Magna Carta ... Holy Grail

live in the moment and stay exclusive, don't make yourself so easily accessible. if people want to get near you, make them do the work. that's how you'll determine who's worthy of your attention. social media has given opportunities to connect with people that would have otherwise been unreachable just by sliding in their dm. people have also become more content with viewing things through their phones instead of living. how many times have you been to a concert and watched it through your phone instead of looking at the stage? how often do you log onto social media and see someone document their entire vacation so much so that you feel as if you were there? when was the last time you saw your best friends, not on social media? while social media definitely has certain benefits, it can compromise the quality of our interactions and experiences. if they want to connect with you, they should find a way to be there.

i am selective about who i spend time and exchange energy with.

march 23
"life's bitch, hope to not make her a widow."
American Dreamin'
American Gangster

the roads of life are full of bumps and can sometimes be challenging to navigate. don't park the car. you owe it to yourself to see it through and allow things to unfold. the thing about life is that your predicament can change in an instant. you've seen it happen for the worse, so don't think for one second that it's impossible for things to change your favor. God doesn't give you anything you can't handle. rise to life's challenges, don't be broken by them.

i persevere.

march 24
"survive the droughts, i wish you well."
American Dreamin'
American Gangster

i'm sure you've heard that tough times create tough people or break people. these times really show what you're made of. they make you reach into your reserves, pull from your investments and force you to get creative on ways to earn to make sure your needs are met. do you have savings? how long will they last you? do you have investments? can you rely on them to support you? if the answer is no, then you should start today. tough times also develop your imagination as you dream about easier days ahead. allow yourself to be refined by the process. plan for the possibility of bad days, hopefully you won't have to implement your plan. if you do, keep fighting through the bad days to get to your best days and let the struggle make you stronger.

i'm sharpened by the struggle.

march 25
"i wish you insight, so you could see for yourself."
American Dreamin'
American Gangster

things are not always as they seem. sometimes, things just are what they are and other times there a deeper meaning. if you're able to let down your guard, defy your preconceived notions and allow yourself to see situations for what they might be your previous experiences may guide you in determining what it is. live life, travel the world, talk to people from all backgrounds, read books and study history to allow yourself to blossom and see the world through a different lens. having insight offers you clarity in your assessments and decision-making.

my vision is clear.

march 26
"maybe i'm the one, or maybe i'm crazy."
Marcy Me
4:44

who do you think you are? seriously, think for a second and answer honestly. does what you think align with what you say and how you act? are you confident or do you constantly second guess who you are and get in your own way? be crazy enough to believe in yourself even if no one else does. forget what they think, they probably don't believe in themselves. and if you don't believe in yourself, why should anyone else? you may get some crazy stares and you may hear some crazy talk, but they are just tests to make sure you believe. don't be controlled by others' opinions of you. keep doing you and let them keep up. don't stop believing. let your thoughts match your words, your words match your actions and watch it all be reflected in your outcomes. become your wildest dreams.

i'm a believer.

march 27
"think i didn't see the lame sneaking' in the back door. it's aight he can come here, for real. you aight, but i'm done here."
I Don't Wanna Be Alone -Remix (Shai)

when you elevate, you have to be especially careful of the company you keep. there are just some places you should not be and some people you should not be around. when you have something to lose, there is no reason to keep company with those that have nothing to lose. they will test you and potentially put you in compromising positions, simply because you can. simply because they have access to you. you will be tempted to stand your ground, but why? you have nothing to prove to people that have done nothing. don't risk the things that you've worked so hard for to prove that you're hard. avoid these situations by steering clear of these people. if they come where you are, excuse yourself. you can't control their actions, but you most certainly can control yours. move around when clowns come around unless you want to be a part of the circus.

i elevate myself and my surroundings.

march 28
"if imma make it to a billi i can't take the same route."
Oceans
Magna Carta ... Holy Grail

there is a saying that the definition of insanity is to keep doing the same thing expecting different results. habits can be hard to break and it's easy to take the mindset that "this is just how i am." society has somehow encouraged the idea that change is a bad thing although change is a part of life. change is a byproduct of growth and if you are not growing then you are not living. growth offers new perspectives and opens new doors. embrace change, embrace growth, and step forward toward your goals. don't be hindered by your refusal to step out of your comfort zone. if you want something you've never had before, you have to do something you've never done. change what you're doing to get better results.

i live outside of my comfort zone.

march 29
"i crash thru glass ceilings, i break through closed doors."
Oceans
Magna Carta ... Holy Grail

it can be hard to play a game that you didn't create the rules to, especially if you don't understand the rules. even harder when it feels like the game is rigged because the rules appear to constantly be changing. it can feel like doors keep slamming in your face after you've worked so hard to unlock them. so, you'll have to be creative to stay competitive and stay motivated. don't allow a seemingly difficult path to discourage you. figure out the cheat codes in the game. instead of thinking outside of the box, realize that there is no box, and it is what you say it is. be inspired by your vision and be confident in your abilities to make things happen. surprise the naysayers, inspire the dreamers and prove yourself right. do the things that you know, deep down, you're capable of.

i have no limits.

march 30
"turned the whole city on, i'm the new plug."
Oh My God
Kingdom Come

representing where you come from isn't just about rooting for the local sports teams, wearing hats with your city on it, or still living in the city that you were born in. it's about what you give back to the city that made you. have gone back to your elementary school to volunteer? high school? do you litter the streets or do your part to clean them up? do you feed the hungry or fault them? do you help people or hurt them? are you putting people to work? are you putting people on? are you connecting the dots? what do your actions say about how you really feel about the city that raised you?

i put on for my city.

march 31
"what didn't kill me, make me strong as i am."
Oh My God
Kingdom Come

life happens.
what's important is not what happens to you, but how your rise from it. you must know that you're stronger than the things that happen to you. think about the tough times that you've overcome. what about the rough moments that you never thought you'd make it through?
life's challenges are pop quizzes testing and strengthening you to help you better manage the weight on your shoulders. give it all you got and keep rising to the top. work on your muscle memory, so the things thrown your way seem to get easier but realize that you really getting stronger. you've got this.

i am strong because of what i've survived.

april 1
"i'm feeling like the worlds against me god, call me crazy but strangely i love the odds."
Oh My God
Kingdom Come

of course, it's easier to win the game when the crowd is rooting for you and the referee is ruling in your favor. conversely, it's discouraging to be to be taunted and feel like you don't know the rules. you are playing at a disadvantage. but imagine how rewarding it will be to still win with everyone and everything working against you and rooting for your failure. now, that's something to be proud of. don't let this crazy world get to you and force you to give up on the things you want most. you owe it to yourself to win. winners win... so, win.

i will win against all odds.

april 2
"push thru the pain so we can see new life."
Smile
4:44

have you ever seen a woman give birth? even if not in real life, i'm sure you've seen it in movies. these women appear to be in such pain and exemplify tremendous strength as they continue to literally push forward to bring a life into the world. when the pressure gets to be too much, what do they do? breathe. take notes from these women that give life every single day. if they stopped pushing, life as we know it would cease. face your pain in anticipation of something new and better than what you have known until this point because it is a result of the best parts you. move forward with new clarity from the lessons from past hurts.

i face my pain to see my power.

april 3
"bet before i go i put a million on the board."
Smile
4:44

what did you come into the world with? nothing. so, there is nowhere for you to go but up. get in the game and shoot your shot and keep shooting. you may not have control over how long you're here on this earth, but it is most certainly up to you to make your time count. what do you consider winning? how do you want to be remembered? write it down. make a plan. get to work and don't stop until you get it.

i won't stop until the game is over.

april 4
"i mastered my aesthetics."
Smile
4:44

people do judge books by their covers. it's up to you to make sure the content of your character is even more impressive than your exterior. let your beauty on the outside merely be a trailer for the depths of beauty on the inside. you don't have to be adorned in designers to make a statement. the way God made you is better than any designer you can wear. you are a work of art and that should be reflected on every level of your being. confidently project an image that authentically reflects, not only, who you are, but also, the person you intend to become. know yourself and use your lifetime to master self.

i practice self-mastery.

april 5
“a loss ain’t a loss it’s a lesson. appreciate the pain it’s a blessing.”
Smile
4:44

understand that we are being improved through what may feel like punishment. as an athlete or student, when you lose a game or fail a test do you review the tape or check you work to see where you went wrong? will you be better prepared for the next game or the next exam? life will continue testing you until you pass. take your lessons and move forward with grace and confidence. pain changes you, but make sure you’re allowing it to change you for the better. don’t become bitter as a result of life’s lessons. we all go through things and jump through hoops to learn our lessons and push us into our greatness.

life’s lessons have made me better.

april 6
"a man that don't take care of his family can't be rich."
Family Feud
4:44

do you do your part to protect and provide for your family? honestly, do you take care of your family in the same way, or better, than you take care of yourself? to be rich is to live a life of abundance. a man's role has historically been as the provider and protector. the hunter. while a woman's role naturally has been as the nurturer. with the women's rights movement the lines associated with responsibilities designated by gender roles begun to blur, but the fact is that all the responsibilities need to be fulfilled regardless of who on the team fills the role. yes, team. scientifically, both male and a female are required to create life, so both need to fulfill the responsibilities to raise one.

i put family first.

april 7
"my consciousness was michael's common sense."
Family Feud
4:44

you came into the world a blank slate. you knew nothing about people, places, things or the world in general. we all have a learning curve, and it is different for different people. over time, your experiences, education and upbringing should allow you to form logical thoughts. however, just because you've learned some things, you cannot expect that the rest of the world must now be equipped with the same learnings that you have. the world is not on your schedule. remember, there was a time when you didn't know the things that you know now, but others did. show some compassion, offer some understanding and approach situations with perspective and pass on the knowledge you've gained instead of being condescending.

i am constantly learning and evolving.

april 8
"we all lose when the family feuds."
Family Feud
4:44

your family is the team you've been assigned to by god. you're bound together whether you like them or not. have you ever argued with a family member and witnessed that disagreement affect the rest of the family? these disagreements can make holiday gatherings uncomfortable or even break up entire households. different personalities, conflicting values and various misunderstandings can all play a part. think about the popular game show where members from one family compete against another family. regardless of what those family members may have going on personally, they work together on the show to get the reward. imagine if one of family's getting sidetracked by a petty argument between two of the members that ultimately disqualifies the family from the game. focus on the big picture, resolve your differences for the benefit of everyone.

i maintain healthy relationships with my family for my family.

april 9
"we all screwed cause we never had the tools."
Family Feud
4:44

we come here as empty vessels and our parents fill us with the knowledge and experience, we need to allow us to navigate the world and build our empire. unfortunately, many of our parents have nothing tangible of value for us to inherit and they inadvertently pass on the miseducation that resulted in their inability to accumulate wealth. they spent their lives trying to build a foundation, leaving us with no shelter in challenging times. while we have proven that we can stand the rain, we've done little to build the house. even worse, we've started to furnish it and fill the closets because it's easier to accumulate the things with no value that require no discipline or sacrifice. so, when it rains, it pours. we still don't seem to know how to build the house any more than our parents did? we have to overcome the disadvantages that our parents faced and begin educating ourselves in this Information Age and focus on building our empires so that our kids won't have to start from nothing and continue to face the same challenges.

i collect tools to construct my dreams.

april 10
“you got the shit that niggas die for. Why you mad? Take the good with the bad.”
Holy Grail
Magna Carta ... Holy Grail

someone else is praying for the things that you take for granted. in fact, you may have once prayed for those same things you disregard. wake up every day with a grateful heart and a motivated mind. have you ever prayed for a particular job, gotten the job, and immediately started to complain regularly about everything from the commute to your co-workers? it’s funny how we disregard that we are now able to support ourselves and our families because of this job, which was the reason we wanted it anyway. have you ever hoped for a boyfriend or girlfriend, but then start to start unnecessary arguments over insignificant things? have you hoped for a new car, but then complain about having to fill it with gas? everything won’t always be all good or all bad. you’ve gotta know how to navigate both and appreciate the good times and become better in the bad.

i understand that life consists of good and bad.

april 11
"if fear is your only god, then to get y'all to fear me is my only job."
Crown
Magna Carta... Holy Grail

what do you fear? the things you fear hold power of you and can prevent you from doing the things you are drawn to. do you want to see the world but have a fear of flying? do you want to live your life but have a fear of dying? the fear that you feel is not real and can be overcome with your own thoughts. the easiest way to overcome your fears is to just push through it and do it. once you done it, not only will you realize that you are bigger than your fears, but you will also start to gain strength and confidence in yourself that will inspire you to try new things and face other things that you were once fearful of. everything you want is on the other side of your fears. don't let your self-inflicted fears stall your progress or prevent you from living your best life.

i fear nothing.

april 12
“too much enemy fire to catch a friendly.”
Murder To Excellence
Watch The Thrown

can you imagine being on an athletic team and having your shots blocked by your teammates and the opposing team? crazy, right? are your friends supportive of you or are they sabotaging you? are you encouraging your friends or are you acting like their enemy? do you make jokes at your friends’ expense? are you operating in love or in malice? are you saying and doing things behind your friends backs that you would never say or to their faces? it’s too many people out here against you for you to be taken down by someone that you call a friend. be clear on who you’re dealing with. are these your friends or your enemies? don’t only consider how people are interacting with you but hold yourself accountable and pay attention to what energy you’re giving off. friendship requires reciprocity and so does enmity. make sure you’re putting out what you are getting and vice versa.

i am friendly to my friends.

april 13
"strays from the same shade, nigga we on the same team. giving you respect, i expect the same thing."
Murder To Excellence
Watch The Throne

what is the epitome of the "crabs in a barrel" mentality? instead of working together to get out of the barrel and bring down the person that put you in there, you'd rather focus your efforts on tripping each other up so you can be the first or only one out. whether in or out of the barrel, you're still a crab. if you get out, you'll be the only one of your kind free, or at the best, the minority, because all the other crabs are still trying to fight their way out. making it out doesn't necessarily make you special. it makes you a deserter if you kicked down the door and closed it behind you. and everyone on both sides knows it. that's why they don't trust or respect you. assumedly, if you'd do that to your own kind, heaven only knows what you would do to them. alternatively, if we work together to tip the barrel over, we could bum rush the scene. we can only do so little ourselves, but together our impact could be immeasurable.

i will not play against my team.

april 14
"real niggas just multiply."
Murder to Excellence
Watch The Throne

when the people we love transition out of this world we feel a tremendous loss because we'll never have an opportunity to see or speak to them again. while that may be true in the traditional sense, i believe that their loss now requires us to be a little more creative in our recognition of their presence. think about the impact that they've left on the world. all the people that attended their home going and shared memories about them. those memories never die and neither does their impact. have you ever had a conversation with someone and found yourself expressing a sentiment that was shared with you or learned from the loved one you lost? i know i have and i recognize those moments as that person having planted their seed with me as i'm sure they'd done with so many others while they were here. they've left pieces of themselves with everyone they've touched while they were alive and with all of those that will be impacted by their love and their light.

i look for my loved ones that passed away in my lessons.

april 15
"if you put crabs in a barrel to ensure your survival you gon' end up pulling down niggas that look just like you."
Murder To Excellence
Watch The Throne

do you want to see others do well? even in times when you are not? do you feel threatened or motivated others are doing better than you? is your mentality... 'if i can't have it, neither can you"? this attitude prevents us from progressing. you have to see the value in rooting for other's rise. if one of us wins, it creates opportunities for us all in the big picture. stop thinking small. come together, or at least don't attempt to block another's blessings. two heads are better than one, so the probability of lasting success is more likely when you decide to work together. stop working against people that have the same overarching goal as you. if we all want to be free, let's combine our strength and work as a team to break the chains. it suits you to work together. there is power in numbers.

the barrel is not my natural habitat.

april 16
“only spot a few blacks the higher i go. what’s up to will. shout out to o. that ain’t enough, we gon need a million more.”
Murder To Excellence
Watch The Throne

are you a minority at work? what about where you hang out? is there an obvious difference in who you’re surrounded by socially and professionally? why do you think that is? have you ever tried socializing outside of your comfort zone? did the place have wardrobe restrictions for entry that seemed to be associated with excluding trends from a particular culture, but once you got in the music was fueled by the very people they were trying to exclude? stop trying to ride the wave, when you and people like you, provide the wave. don’t think you are special because you were actually allowed in. consider that maybe you were just seen as less threatening. stay on their necks. come together with other special ones and kick down the door, and make sure it stays open for other deserving souls that add to the energy.

as i progress, i assist others in their progression.

april 17
"niggas is fronting that's upside-down cake get em a red nose they clown cakes."
Pound Cake / Paris Morton Music 2 (Feat. JAY-Z)
Nothing Was The Same (Deluxe) by Drake

clowns paint on ridiculous faces and perform for others entertainment. they do the silliest things to get people's attention, even if it is to be laughed at. how ridiculous does that sound when you really take time to consider it? they'll intentionally trip and fall, take pies in the face and other unfortunate occurrences to impress others. be yourself and the right people will like you. if you have to take losses and change who you are for others, then they don't deserve you. and if you're willing to change who you are for the amusement of others; you need to take a closer look in the mirror and evaluate why you don't like yourself. be genuine. be authentic. be real. be you. everyone else is already taken, just focus on being yourself.

it ain't no future in my fronting.

april 18
"i den made more millionaires then the lotto did."
Pound Cake / Paris Morton Music 2 (Feat. JAY-Z)
Nothing Was The Same (Deluxe) by Drake

the realest thing you can do is put others in a position to make money. money is currency and, in this world, money allows you to feed, clothe, and house yourself and your family. in capitalist societies, all of things needed for survival demand payment. if you're making money, then you likely are in a position to do business with others. are you hoarding away your earnings? or are you freely exchanging funds for services? are you helping developing others' ideas and talents to allow them an opportunity to thrive, as well? if not, you need to ask yourself why. are you threatened by others' success? do you want to be the only earner? are you a hater? if the latter, get your shit together. spread love and share the wealth. adopt the 'when i eat you eat' mentality and there will be a surplus of food. it's enough to go around.

my wealth produces wealth for others.

april 19
"i told him less is more nigga it's plenty of us."
Pound Cake / Paris Morton Music 2 (Feat. JAY-Z)
Nothing Was The Same (Deluxe) by Drake

would you rather have 10 lions or 100 sheep? focus less on how many people you are surrounded by and more on the quality of the people in your circle. how good are the people you surround yourself with? how much influence do they have? in order to be an effective leader, you must have followers. in order to be a boss, you must have workers. the few can influence the masses if they recognize their reach. what are you doing with your power? are you putting people to work? are you educating people? what are you doing to put people on? to allow them to improve their predicament and make them better? focus on the impact.

i value quality over quantity.

april 20
"i look in the mirror, my only opponent."
Welcome To The Jungle
Watch The Throne

each morning when you awake set out to be a better person than you were the day before. each day is an opportunity to get it right and be a better version of yourself. that's why you shouldn't spend any real time beating yourself up for mistakes you may have made. mistakes are just missteps, so with the new day, hit the reset button and take steps with intention using the insight from lessons learned and proceed with a hopeful and determined mindset. break the limits that you previously set for yourself. outgrow your old self. replace your bad habits with better ones. you are not in competition with other people. just outdo the old you.

i am better than i was yesterday.

april 21
“you can turn up your nose high society, never gone turn down the homie.”
Somewhereinamerica
Magna Carta... Holy Grail

you are not defined by other people’s opinions of you. don’t concern yourself with fitting in. ignore the judgment. focus on what’s special about you and remain determined. don’t validate the limitations that others try to impose upon you. their limits are not your limits. don’t give in and start to believe that you’re not good enough, as tempting as it might be to believe the bad things. try, for once. to believe only the good things that have been said about you and that you believe about yourself. most times people’s judgements are uninformed. they don’t really know you, so how can they judge you? besides, who are they to judge? you’ll be judged no matter what, so you may as well believe the things you say about yourself above all.

i will not be shut down or shut out.

april 22
"look a man dead in his eyes so he know you talk truth when you speak it, give your word? keep it."
New Day
Watch The Throne

mean what you say and say what you mean. these days, people say things without ever expecting to be held accountable for what they've said. people hastily speak in anger, excitement, and boredom. they even say things to be liked. if you speak for any reason other than expressing your truth, you are likely compromising the validity of your statements. not only do words have power but they can leave powerful impressions and resonate with people long after they have been said. consider the impact of dr. martin luther king jr.'s "i have a dream" speech. do you remember hateful or critical words spoken to you from your youth? also, you probably remember every broken promise. prove yourself to be a reliable resource. your word should be your bond. you begin to lose credibility when you don't keep your word. it's quite simple, if you don't know it to be true, don't speak it. the truth is not situational.

i speak the truth.

april 23
"promise to never leave him even if his momma tweaking, cause my dad left me and I promise never repeat him."
New Day
Watch The Throne

most of your intimate relationships have probably been temporary. for one reason or another the relationship came to an end regardless of whether you had the best of intentions. imagine if each of those relationships resulted in a life being brought into this world. now, a child is here that didn't ask to be here anymore than you did. a child whose self-worth will be determined by how much his parents pour into him and the quality of the love and information that he is given. imagine being forced to play a professional sport with no coach, or teammates. you'd be a significant disadvantage, wouldn't you? imagine being the coach and carelessly putting players in the game and deciding to not coach them because your assistant coach pissed you off, but still expecting them to win. crazy, right? the goal is to be better to your children than your parents were to you. if your parents weren't around, be who you needed as a child. if your parents were good, be great.

i love and nurture my children.

april 24
"sins of a father make your life ten times harder."
New Day
Watch The Throne

growing up, how often did you hear "are you so-and-so's son?" or "you look just like your mother." that recognition may have opened some doors for you, and in some cases may have shut them. the things you have and haven't done, what and who you know and don't know all impact the lives of your children. it fuels your perspective and what you're able to pass on to them. how you've lived your life can affect how your children navigate through theirs and how they're judged by their peers and gatekeepers. there will come a time when you'll have to share your past grievances with your children as either a learning opportunity or in a moment of truth. operate in transparency and be equipped with the lessons from your ills so you are telling your story from a 'been there, done that, learn this' perspective so they won't have to. don't fake perfection. live in your truth and share your lessons.

i make my child's life easier than mine was.

april 25
"cause when my backs against the wall, nigga, i react."
Say Hello
American Gangster

how do you respond to pressure? do you fold, or do you rise to the challenge? do you allow yourself to be bullied or do you stand ten toes down? do you give up when you seemingly have no other options, or do you get creative? flex your mental and physical muscles to create opportunities for yourself. if you're alive, you've got options, so do get discouraged and don't ever give up. it literally isn't over until it's over. each waking hour is an opportunity to devise a plan, revise the plan and work the plan. you've gotta make things happen for yourself. your life and your livelihood are depending on you to take control.

i will not be boxed in.

april 26
"me and destiny got a date."
F.U.T.W.
Magna Carta... Holy Grail

you are destined for greatness. although life may happen and challenges may occur to make your journey more colorful, it is up to you to pursue the things that are meant for you. what's meant for you is everything you can imagine and some things you can't even begin to fathom. don't be discouraged by the journey, be sharpened by it. everything that happens to you makes you stronger and, in turn, makes your story more interesting. you're the author of your own story and it's up to you how it turns out. how bad do you want the things that you have imagined for yourself? don't give up. keep going. show up every day. you've got things to do, places to go and people to meet. let's goooooo!

i cannot be stopped.

april 27
"we have yet to see a ceiling, we just top what we top. cause the bars don't struggle and the struggle don't stop."
F.U.T.W.
Magna Carta... Holy Grail

you are your only limitation. have you ever been working out and thought that you couldn't go any further and decided to push yourself a little bit more because your health and fitness goals are a priority? you were pretty surprised at yourself, weren't you? this small win probably allowed you to approach your next workout with added confidence and bigger goals because you wanted to challenge your accomplishment from the last time. it's all in your mind. you can go further, workout harder, think bigger and earn more if you first believe that you are capable and commit to do what is required to get to the next level.

i shatter glass ceilings.

april 28
"1 percent of a billion more than niggas ever seen, still they wanna act like it's an everyday thing."
F.U.T.W.
Magna Carta... Holy Grail

do you hate from outside of the club? i'm sure you've seen it. of course, you've heard people talk about how a club or restaurant that they've never been to is wack. how they don't like someone that they've never met. how someone else is stupid for making a deal for more than their salary over multiple years. these people seem to have strong opinions about things that they haven't even come close to experiencing and therefore, know very little about. instead of refraining from commenting or at the very least, using these situations as opportunities to research so that they might intelligently give their two cents. would you rather have 100% of $60,000 or 1% of $1,000,000,000? either way, both of are worth more than your 2 cents. congratulate the winners, no matter what place they come in, and sit back and take notes.

i only speak on things i know about.

april 29
"i just want a shot to show my genius, standing on the top hold my penis."
F.U.T.W.
Magna Carta... Holy Grail

there is something that you are great at. you might be overlooking it because it comes easy to you. your talent is a gift that is given to you by God. open your gift and realize that it's up to you to provide the batteries. it is your job to figure out what it is and share it with the world. don't be complacent with being average, be great. stop lurking in other's shadows, step into the sunshine and join the winner's circle. winning requires talent and showcasing that talent requires confidence. don't always be thinking what-if. how many people do you know that can sing or dance but are too shy to show others for fear that they will be judged? what comes easy to you? what do you enjoy doing? i'm sure someone is making a lucrative living from those very things. don't let your talents waste away. show us what you've got.

i shoot my shot.

april 30
"tell him rumble young man rumble, try to dim your lights tell you be humble."
F.U.T.W.
Magna Carta... Holy Grail

no matter what you do or have done, there will always be people that criticize you, judge you or try to knock you down. the only way to avoid criticism is to do absolutely nothing, but you'll still be called lazy. expect the critics. be worried if you don't have them. prove them wrong. do what they said you could not do. prove the people that believe in you right. don't be discouraged by the people that feel it's their place to put you in your place. who are they to decide where your place is in this world? you've got ambition, baby. be your own motivation, despite the hate mail. greet them with determination. believe that you are the greatest! who cares if no one else believes in you if you believe in yourself? you don't need a fan club. share your talents with the world and know that you deserve everything you've gotten and everything that's coming.

i shine bright.

may 1
"you know i'm gone shine like a trillion watts."
F.U.T.W
Magna Carta... Holy Grail

you know that confidence you have when you're at home in the mirror? That feeling that you're untouchable. Take that into the world! Just like with the sun, your light may shine so brightly that it may take some getting used to for others. They won't know what to do with you. that's okay rise every day and light up the world. Let them adjust to your shine. Keep shining.

i will not allow others to dim my light.

may 2
"little bastard boy, basking on top."
F.U.T.W
Magna Carta... Holy Grail

where you come from does not define you, nor does it determine where you're going. you have no control over where you're placed in this world or the circumstances you are born into. whether you're born rich, or poor is not up to you. whether your parents stick around to raise you or avoid their responsibilities and abandon you ... still not up to you. what is up to you is how you play the hand that you were dealt. Are you going to win or are you going to fold? Play that hand like it is exactly what you would've hoped for and win! Make the world wonder how you've done it.

i will succeed despite my circumstances.

may 3
"teacher teacher, try to unteach ya, all the shit they taught ya that got ya all in the bleachers."
F.U.T.W
Magna Carta... Holy Grail

how much have you learned as an adult that left you wondering why you were never taught these things in school? the clarifier to the 13th amendment. the i have a dream speech in its entirety. politics. you quickly realize that you've been miseducated. all the things you were taught took the fight out of you. left you sitting on the sidelines watching instead of making thing happen. it's up to you to continue educating yourself and correct the misinformation you've been given so freely. do your own research, then figure out who benefits from your being misinformed and you'll be clear on who benefits from you being informed. you're responsible for your own salvation, so get to work.

i will not watch from the sidelines when i'm meant to play the game.

may 4
"make a million of a million, let my niggas make a million, till we all check a billion, shit it's just the way i'm feeling."
F.U.T.W
Magna Carta... Holy Grail

is there only one person in your crew that is successful. is it you? does everyone else serve as hype men for the successful one? if so, find a new crew. make sure everyone knows how to fish. if someone is blocking you from making money, saving money, investing money or not allowing you blatant opportunities to do so despite your being qualified and prepared, they are not your friend. if you are the one doing the blocking, then you are no friend. let the wealth spread like wildfire.

i am a team player.

may 5
"put in the belly of the beast, i escaped a nigga never had a job."
Crown
Magna Carta... Holy Grail

it is true that what doesn't kill you only makes you stronger, if you allow it. think about the things that you have experienced throughout your life that you thought you would never make it through. now, look at you. you might've suffered a few bumps and bruises, but you survived and you're stronger and smarter as a result. what you've been through has probably made what you will go through seem like a walk in the park. stop thinking that things are getting easier for you, when, in reality, you've gotten stronger. you may not have gotten the experience you needed in a manner that you'd preferred, but you got a lot of hands-on lessons that have ensured that you won't break when pressure is applied. take pride in your strength. put those muscles to work.

i'm a fighter.

may 6
"best friends become ya enemies, niggas' knives are double-edged."
Crown
Magna Carta... Holy Grail

you've lost friends throughout your life that you thought would always be around. they probably told some secrets that you thought were in the vault. they might have two-timed you in a way that you would never had thought possible of someone that you loved. the lesson is to pay closer attention to whether someone is exhibiting the qualities of an ally or an enemy. people pretend well, but they always have slips. if you were paying attention, you wouldn't have dismissed certain things and deemed them insignificant. just because you hang around someone doesn't mean they're for you. just because someone says they have your back; doesn't mean they actually will when put to the test. life will always expose weak bonds, so you've got to tune in.

i separate my friends from my foes.

may 7
"if fear is your only god, to get y'all to fear me is my only job."
Crown
Magna Carta... Holy Grail

what do you fear? remember when you were afraid of the dark? were you afraid of monsters under your bed or in the closet? maybe you were afraid of dogs or heights. it turns out that you may have just been afraid of the unknown. once you faced your fear, you learned that it wasn't so scary, after all. if you succumb to your fears, they will always have power over you. in fact, if you make others aware of your fears, they will also have power over you. just like you did with the darkness, the monsters under your bed, and your neighbors' little dog, be courageous and conquer your fears. you'll begin to feel a freedom and confidence that you once thought was impossible. it is life-changing to face your fears as you'll see all the possibilities. don't hesitate. again, what do you fear?

i have no fear.

may 8
“niggas always try to knock a nigga down, knocked me to my knees about a million times.”
Crown
Magna Carta... Holy Grail

it is a given that if you’re doing well, there will always be people that try stop your progress. don’t be discouraged. keep going. think of life like a boxing match. it ain’t over ‘til it’s over. just because you got knocked down, doesn’t mean you shouldn’t keep working to get on your feet and keep swinging. it’s okay to get knocked down as long as you get up. it’s all a part of the process, it may even give you an opportunity to breathe. don’t waste your valuable time feeling sorry for yourself and crying about getting knocked down. use your down time as a moment to get your mind right and get back up with a fresh perspective. you’ve got to always get back up.

i always get up.

may 9
"uncle said i'd never sell a million records, i sold a million records like a million times."
Crown
Magna Carta... Holy Grail

when people doubt your ability to do something, it's not always because they are hating on you. they weren't given your vision, nor were they given your talent. how can you expect them to see something that was specifically created for you? you're expecting them to visualize and believe in something that's bigger than their imagination. it's likely that they will shoot down your dreams because they've never been able to fly that high. to them, you are in dangerous territory, a no-fly zone. don't get mad, just be careful with who you share your dreams with. once you realize that someone doesn't have the capacity to dream with you, stop. i'm sure you've already thought of a million reasons it may fail; you can only afford to be encouraged. be cautious with your dreams, they're extremely precious.

i dream in color and some people are colorblind.

may 10
"once a good girls gone bad, she's gone forever.
Song Cry
The Blueprint

relationships are complex. to give a relationship a fair chance it requires both people to put their absolute trust in the other and allow yourself to be vulnerable. many people are guarded for so many reasons, including their upbringing and prior relationships. generally, once someone has been broken as a result of a relationship gone bad, every future relationship becomes more challenging as a result of their trauma. You think you're recognizing patterns that may just be paranoia and insecurity. it may be unrealistic to expect people to treat each relationship individually. throughout life people generally take their lessons from experiences and use that information to intelligently navigate life. relationships are no different. leave people better than you found them. be careful with others' hearts. if you don't have your own traumas and trust issues resolved, don't disrupt someone else's peace and traumatize them.

i am good to good people.

may 11
“people keep talking about "Hov take it back"! i'm doing better than before why would i do that?”
What We Talkin' About
The Blueprint 3

there is this idea that if you change you aren’t being authentic. everything in life changes. everything. yet, somehow, you are expected to be the same person at 30 that you were at 15, and at 40 that you were at 20 and so on. for that to true, that would mean that you have not evolved or grown. what a waste of time. and all to appease another person’s idea of who you are and who you should be. imagine that. can you stand behind every decision you made when you were younger? if so, you were either really evolved at a young age or you may be really stupid at an old age. make choices for your life that contribute to your growth and progression. edit yourself until it feels right, and when you’re inclined to do so, edit again. it’s your life and you only have one. don’t be defined by or confined to your past because others have placed you in a cage. keep going and keep growing.

i move upward and onward.

may 12
"how could you ever destroy the beauty from which one came, that's a savage."
Lucky Me
In My Lifetime... Vol 1

for nine months, your mom shared her body with you and nourished and protected you to allow you to develop into a fresh. can you imagine the selflessness that it takes to literally share your body with another? some people won't even share their food. to allow someone to grow inside of you, to your discomfort, is an amazing sacrifice and representation of love that guarantees no reciprocity. you know the sound of her heart beating from the inside. the sound of her life. consider the neighborhoods that raised you and provided protection. how do you show gratitude to your parents, to your environment, to all of the people and things that conspired to get you where you are today? or do you just take and contribute to the destruction of those things and people with your bad vibes and bad actions? check yourself.

i live civil and operate in love.

may 13
"they talk, we live"
What We Talkin' About
The Blueprint 3

how do you spend your time? are you always talking about what you want to do or are you doing it? are you daydreaming about what you could have and should have done or are you actually doing. dream while you're asleep and wake up and live. talking about your dreams is the easy part. everyone can do that because talk is cheap. sometimes, you may talk so much that you may just talk yourself out of the things you dream of. living your dreams takes courage, discipline and direction and this is why actions speak louder than words. so, make some noise! you know what you want! so, don't talk about it, be about it. go after your dreams and make them reality. live your life and get busy making memories and making history.

i'm living.

may 14
"talkin' bout progress i ain't looking back"
What We Talkin' About
The Blueprint 3

each day do you strive to make progress, no matter how small? continuous progress adds up and ultimately results in seeing your goals come to fruition. progress demands change and almost always struggle, so it will require your intense focus. don't be content with how things are if you know they can be better. look forward and do the work to ensure that things become what you want them to be. don't get comfortable. push past your comfort zone and see things come together and thrive. once you begin to see the progression, you'll never again accept anything less and you'll start to wonder what's more. everyday take a step forward, don't willingly take steps back. you should be moving forward with yesterday's lessons that will lead to tomorrow's progression.

i am focused on the future.

may 15
"grown men want me to sit em on my lap
but i don't have a beard and santa claus ain't black."
What We Talkin' About
The Blueprint 3

you are responsible for you. if you know how to fish, you will never be hungry. sitting around with your hand out waiting for someone else to feed you is not the way. you will always be at their mercy. who feeds you? if they stopped, would you be hungry? who pays for your housing? if they stopped, would you be homeless? who pays for your clothing? if they stopped, would you be naked? even if you think someone owes you something, be clear that they don't. unless you are a minor or you've figured out a legitimate way to demand your 40 acres, get over it. you are responsible for your own salvation, otherwise you will always be a victim. learn how to swim or you are destined to sink. do yourself a favor and seek out opportunities and stop begging.

i am responsible for my own salvation.

may 16
“and now that that's that let’s talk about the future, we have just seen the dream as predicted by martin luther. and you could choose to sit in front of your computer.”
What We Talkin' About
The Blueprint 3

are you providing the wave or are you riding the wave of the past? don’t get so caught up celebrating yesterday’s win that you’ve become content in the current predicament and foolishly think that the trophy can’t be taken away from you. be clear, the baton has been passed to you, the race was not won. do you think the people that came before us came this far, to only come this far? what are you doing? how are you contributing? are you contributing? or are you just reaping the benefits and the blessings and fucking things up for those that will come after you? are you posing in the shot feeling yourself forgetting that the rest of the game still needs to be played? are you a dreamer or a dream-snatcher? don’t turn the dream into a nightmare, get to work.

i am my ancestors’ wildest dreams.

may 17
"you stuck on being hardcore i chuck the deuce up."
What We Talkin' About
The Blueprint 3

being a tough guy doesn't mean that you're strong. it means that you feel you have something to prove to others, and it just might mean that you are the weakest link. don't leave yourself wide open for people to test you. what else do you have going on besides your bravado? what are you accomplishing? are you in rooms where you have to be hardcore? maybe you're in the wrong rooms. are you the bully on the playground? it might be time to grow up. are you a social media gangster? log off. there are bigger things in the world than playing a tough guy role. focus on getting through tough times and becoming mentally tough.

may 18
“what do you do when the love turns the hate?”
Why I Love You
Watch the Throne

love is a daily effort to honor your commitment to a friend, partner or family member. often, love is thought to be a magical, uncontrollable feeling because it can feel that way. you’re not realizing that you are deciding each day, with each interaction that you appreciate someone, their presence and the way they make you feel as a result of their actions. we associate love with our hearts, but it is a feeling that requires us to use our brain to sort through someone’s actions and inaction. when love fades, it’s because we decided that we are no longer seduced by someone and we refuse to continue overlooking their irritants. this can be a result of us growing in different directions, becoming more realistic about the relationship or seeing the person more clearly through an examination of their actions. you decide what to look at, the rose petals or the thorns. you decide if the beauty of the rose is worth the pain of the thorns or if the thorns are too much to bear. be clear about who you are and see people clearly and the love should weather the tests of time.

i will not let my love cloud my judgment.

may 19
"caesar didn't see it so he ceased to assist so the nigga that killed him had keys to his shit."
Why I Love You
Watch the Throne

keep your enemies close and keep your friends closer. that doesn't mean don't trust your friends. what it points out is that sometimes we become so content in how we've designated our relationships that we forget that people can change as circumstances and situations change. you expect to be stricken by your enemy, so you are not surprised when it happens. your friendships offer a sense of comfort, so much so that it weakens your instincts. we fail to pay attention to the behavior patterns of the people close to us, and therefore overlook them when there is a change. we fail to see when their attitudes have shifted because we are stuck reminiscing on memories and ultimately are shocked by their betrayal. you think that a person with seemingly no motive can ever be your enemy. don't allow your oblivious attitude to lead to your downfall.

i am aware of my surroundings.

may 20
"so, i ain't gon' make a move unless i got a plan b."
Trouble
Kingdom Come

are you logical or emotional? if you're both, are you more of one than the other? many people react to their circumstances without thinking about the repercussions of their actions. usually, that only results in making a bad situation worse. would you quit your job without having secured an alternate steam of income? would you give up your apartment without having first found somewhere else to live? so, why don't you use the same logic with other decisions as it relates to your life? don't cut off your nose to spite your face. stop playing checkers and constantly reacting to someone else's move. always think big picture. never forget what the goal is. write it down. make sure that your movements are aligned with that goal. being emotional clouds your judgements and forces your hand to make questionable moves.

i make smart moves.

may 21
"giving you respect; i expect the same thing."
Murder to Excellence
Watch the throne

you must give respect to get respect. treat others the way you want to be treated. if you are showing others respect and they are outwardly disrespecting you be clear on who you are dealing with and adjust how you deal with them. don't be flexible in this. draw your line in the sand and demand your respect as a human being. the absence of boundaries will usually result in the absence of respect, which should result in your absence. be clear that you refuse to tolerate disrespect. if you fail to enforce this, it is perceived as weakness, lack confidence or the lack of self-respect. if you don't first respect yourself, how can you demand that others do what you are unwilling to do? carry yourself with respect and separate yourself from those who don't respect you.

i carry myself with respect.

may 22
“power to the people, when you see me, see you.”
Murder to Excellence
Watch the throne

do you look down on others? do you think you’re better? do you consider yourself more worthy of god’s favor? or do you recognize and accept that we are all children of god? do you understand that until all of us are free, none of us are free? do you recognize the power that lies within us all and respect others as human beings? do you greet others in peace? do you wish them well? do you root for their rise? or do you only hope for your ascent and dream of the days where you can stunt on everyone else? do you want to be better than your people or better with them? think long and hard about that. monitor your thoughts. be careful with your words. check your actions. it all starts with you and your perception of others as it relates to you. if you are constantly putting yourself on a pedestal, you will always be looking down on others.

i am better with others.

may 23
“no answers to these trick questions, no time. shits stressin. my life found, i gotta live for the right now.”
Regrets
Reasonable Doubt

unfortunately, life doesn’t come with an instruction manual. you have to figure it out as you go along and leverage the insights of the people placed in your life to help you navigate. life will keep presenting you with the same test repeatedly in different forms until you get it right. as far as we know, we’ve only got one life to live and we don’t know how much time is in that life, so you have to make decisions and moves that will allow you to live your best life and leave your mark. what do you consider your best life? instagram stunting, club hopping and shopping? or is your best life one that will be remembered for generations to come because you’ve done something impactful? you will forget the names of the nightclubs and be embarrassed by the questionable outfits of the past. but the people you impact with the good that you have done will make sure the world won’t forget your name.

i am mindful and present.

may 24
"one life to live, notice you get no sequel."
Hola Hovito
The Blueprint

when playing video games, you're generally trying to advance as far as the game will allow because when you're done, its game over. what are you doing to get to the next level? are you jumping over the hurdles, avoiding suckers and collecting your rewards? are you making it count! or are you living your life like a bad scary movie. recklessly going through life, tripping over nothing and stumbling to get back up? your life is your movie. make it a classic.

i live every day as if it is my last.

may 25
"pledge allegiance, uh, to my grandma for that banana pudding, our piece of American."
Made in America
Watch the Throne

i'm sure you've heard the saying 'as american as apple pie.' but in your family, you probably rarely ate apple pie, unless it was from mcdonald's. your madear probably baked sweet potato pie or whipped up banana pudding. doesn't your fruit count? ain't you american? if you're of african descent, it's highly likely that your ancestors built america. growing and picking cotton. building railroads. inventing damn near everything and even fighting in the civil war. all of these things literally made america great by putting the country on the map and in a position to be the most powerful country in the world. think about all of the things that have been associated with the country and think about how many of those things represent you. where is your slice of the pie? black history is american history, so show some respect to your great grandparents and their great grandparents and so on and recognize their contributions to the country. salute!

my ancestors made america great.

may 26
"y'all ain't real, that's y'all achilles heel."
Lyrical Exercise
The Blueprint

everyone talks about keeping it real. people will look you in the eye with colored contacts and claim to be real. they will swear on their mother's life and be lying. do you speak the truth, even when its hard? are you being authentically you, even when it's not likeable to others? when you're comfortable being who you are, being transparent with others comes naturally. you are not concerned with others judgement of you because you have accepted yourself and understand that the pieces are a part of your story. good and bad. liars, fronters and all-around characters are constantly putting on costumes and putting on a show to prepare to perform for others to gain their approval. it's easy to pick apart someone that's fake. even to their core the facade reflects weakness within, so their enemies know exactly where to aim. get comfortable with who you are. know your strengths and work on your weakness, so no one will be able to use anything against you.

i am who i am.

may 27
"i look in the mirror, my only opponent."
Welcome to the Jungle
Watch the Throne

do you compete with others or collaborate with them? collaboration is key. in life, the only person you should be competing against is the person you were the day before. push your boundaries. challenge your limits. enhance your strengths. develop your weaknesses. seek opportunities and eliminate threats that interfere with you becoming your best self. if you spend too much time looking at what others are doing, you will take your eye off the ball and put your own goals at risk. stay focused on what's important and hold yourself accountable for what you are to become. if you focus on your improvement and the attainment of your goals, you will understand that what others are doing is of no concern to you.

i am better than i was yesterday.

may 28
"who gon stop me huh?"
Who Gon Stop Me
Watch The Throne

who do you allow to set your limitations? only you can decide how far you go. it's your determination that will take you wherever you decide. there was a movie that i saw in college in which a man's entire life was limited to what others allowed him to see, even in his own home. do you push the boundaries? are you constantly learning? are you always looking for new experiences? do you seek out new places, people and things? if you take some time to think, you may find that it is you that has decided to limit yourself. but why? there is lots of world to see. go see it! there are almost 8 billion people in the world. how many of them have you laid eyes on? how many have you smiled at or said hello to? how many things have you said you wanted to do? how many of them have you done? get out of your own way and get shit done.

i can't stop. i won't stop.

may 29
"where you disappear to son? maintaining. putting myself in a position most of these rappers ain't in."
Feeling it
Reasonable Doubt

someone once told me, "you can't dance to every song or your feet gonna hurt." sometimes you gotta sit down long enough to get a second wind. the culture of social media has caused people to always be craving the spotlight and the attention of others even at the risk of their own livelihood. you can't always ball. you have to be realistic and cutout the lavish spending and take care of your necessities. maintain. stay out of the way. spend less. save more. make more. these things will put you in a better position for your future. do you want to live for a good time or a long time? if you answered both, you have to take yourself off the map sometimes and make sacrifices to ensure your longevity.

i play for the long term.

may 30
"i can't teach you how to stash, see myself i hold cash. every dollar like it's my last, cause it might be."
Broken English & Drug Sellin
Demo

who taught you about money? do you save? invest? spend? give away? where'd you learn your relationship with money? do you think money grows on trees? or do you not know if the money you have might be your last? if your direct deposit didn't come through on your next pay day, do you have a plan? what's your rainy-day fund look like? if this gives you anxiety or if you are somehow confident about where your money comes from despite not having a plan, you need to think again. you might be like most people in that if you don't work, you don't eat. put some money away. if you don't have anything the joke will be on you and i'm sure you won't think it's funny at all. put away some things you need like food, water and money, just in case. hopefully, you'll never need them, but if you do, you'll be glad you were prepared.

i save for the future.

may 31
"please don't die over the neighborhood, that your momma rent in."
The Story Of O.J.
4:44

do you own your home? how about the home you grew up in? is your block, your hood, your city really yours? or can you be forced out by the people that really own and control it? if your neighborhood was gentrified, would you still have your home? if the answer is no, then it is not your hood. ask yourself why don't you own it? how much rent have you paid over the years? enough to by the house that you rent? if you really sacrificed and prioritized ownership and the acquisition of land over being a sneaker head, could you own your home? why do you think having 40 acres was so important? why do you think they refused to distribute it? that is what it means to have a piece of america. if you can be moved at the owner's discretion then you're only visiting.

i will protect what is mine.

june 1
"get your weight up, not your hate up."
Breathe Easy/Lyrical Exercise
The Blueprint

how far have you come from last year? 3 years ago? 5 years ago? 10 years ago? how much have you acquired and accomplished in this time? what's your net worth? $100 or $100,000? do you spend more time talking about other people than you do working on yourself? if so, you're doing it all wrong. every time you get the temptation to talk about someone else, ask yourself what you've done today to work towards your goals. Then, ask yourself what you could be doing that is more productive than gossiping and hating. if you're hating on someone it's probably because they're doing better than you. only you can change that. get to work. make some improvements and make some money. try this, every time you're tempted to gossip do 10 pushups, 25 squats or write or execute the next step of your business plan.

i'm busy working on me.

june 2
"go harder than a nigga for a nigga go figure."
That's My Bitch
Watch The Throne

have you ever heard anyone say, "bros before hoes"? while you should certainly put your family ahead of anyone that you deem a hoe, you should think hard about who you're putting before someone that you've claimed as yours. the time that you're most vulnerable is when you're sleeping. how is it that you can lay next to someone every night with both eyes closed and not show them the loyalty that you offer to your friends? who takes care of you when you're sick? who prepares your food? who do you share your dreams with? who are you building a life with? don't be derailed by sound bites. pay attention to who's holding you down. it doesn't have to be a competition, but i'm sure there is room on your team for someone that supports you and contributes to your growth.

i keep it real with those who keep it real with me.

june 3
"sins of a father make yo life ten times harder."
New Day
Watch The Throne

karma doesn't always come back to the person that committed the bad deed, sometimes it resurfaces for your children and loved ones. just when you think you've gotten away with your bullshit; you are forced to watch loved ones be the recipient of it. make amends. we all detour from our path of greatness at some point. it's up to you to atone your missteps with good deeds as a testament that your life has not been in vain. that your comeback is bigger than your collapse and that everything that has happened was for a reason. it has been said that every saint has a past, and every sinner has a future.

my future is bright.

june 4
"teach ya good values, so you cherish it."
New Day
Watch The Throne

children come into the world a blank canvas. who they become is a result of the lessons that have been poured into them and the experiences they've had. you can't just preach to them to be kind; you have to show them kindness. you can't tell them to work hard if all they see is you sitting on your ass being unproductive. you can't tell them to give back if they only see taking. not only will young people grow to be the epitome of the values that have been instilled in them, they will grow to expect those same values from others and will not tolerate anything less. kids can't raise themselves and if they're forced to, they become adults that lack values, morals, self-esteem and direction. your children will not become good people by accident. you can't water a seed with soda and place it in darkness and expect it to flourish.

i owe it to my children to raise them.

june 5
"took me twenty-six years to find my path.
my only job is cutting the time in half."
New Day
Watch The Throne

how long did it take you to figure out what you wanted to do with your life? how long did it take you to learn the lessons that you've been lucky enough to learn. as you speak to other people you find out that those lessons are not especially unique although the circumstances that brought them may have been. don't waste the precious time that the young people in your life have. allow them the benefit of learning from your mistakes. don't try to appear perfect, tell them what it took for you to come to the revelation. allow them to experience things that will open their minds to the things that develop and encourage their talents. their course in life should be much easier than yours because you already know where most of the bumps are. the world is hard enough, make sure you're not making it harder for them. give them the advantages that you weren't blessed to have so the blessings can continue to flow for generations.

i'll leave crumbs for my child to follow.

june 6
"look a man dead in his eyes so he know you talk truth when you speak it, give your word, keep it."
New Day
Watch the Throne

how irritating is when you're having an in-person conversation with someone and they are looking everywhere but at you. even more frustrating when you've been trying to make eye contact the entire conversation. the failure to make eye contact can make you question a person's intentions or question the validity of things that they speak about. what can possibly be more important and demanding of your attention than the words that you have selected to speak and the person you have chosen to speak to? or do you just like to hear yourself talk? as a child, do you remember an occasion when your parent was speaking to you and paused to say "look at me" before making a strong statement or giving important directions? you knew they meant business, right? take note.

i demand undivided attention.

june 7
"i just pray we was in love on the night that we conceived him."
New Day
Watch The Throne

sex is a very intimate experience. it is literally a physical opportunity for two people to become one, fitting together like puzzle pieces. it is also the only natural way to conceive. consider what has to happen for conception to occur. millions of sperm are released, and one wins the lottery to create a human. wow. look at those odds. all of that energy went into creating you. imagine what an emotional advantage you could have if you were conceived in love versus being conceived in indifference or in hate. be aware of your feelings for a person when you are risking the possibility of conception. a child is a half of you and a half of the other person. is it possible to fully love a child if you never loved both parties that are reflected in that child? do you love yourself? do you love your partner? a child can have characteristics of either parent. how do you unconditionally love someone that is a spitting image of someone you hate? be thoughtful and do all things in love.

i nurture all things that comes from me.

june 8
"promise to never leave him even if his mama tweaking', cause my dad left me and i promise never repeat him."
New Day
Watch The Throne

some of us had the misfortune of growing up without both of our parents due to our parents' inability to be or to choose a responsible partner or because of one or both of our parents' unwillingness to co-parent. these things that had absolutely nothing to do with you and were beyond your control impacted your life and emotional wellbeing and affected the adult you would become. the truth is, our parents' decisions, action and inaction, affect our stability and our self-worth, just as their parents' actions influenced them. break the curse. you know what didn't feel right and what you never want to feel again. conversely, you know what you longed for. becoming a parent is your opportunity to duplicate what you felt your parents did right and correct what you felt they did wrong. be a better version of your parents, so your child can be a better version of you.

i will be who i needed as a child.

june 9
“build your fences, we digging' tunnels.”
Otis
Watch The Throne

fences are erected to keep people out or to be a deterrent to allow people to freely exit. first, you need to figure out why the fence is there and decide what side of the fence it makes for sense for you to be on. also, understand that all fences cannot be seen. either way, don’t allow these obstructions to force you to give up on your goals. find another way. you may find that the alternative might be a better route. if you can’t walk through the fence, maybe you can climb over it or crawl under it. harriet tubman used the underground railroad to allow enslaved people to escape hellish slave plantations in the pursuit of freedom. stay motivated, be persistent and be courageous. be confident in your position and know that no one can stop what is for you if you don’t allow it. make a choice.

i can’t be stopped.

june 10
"all i got is dreams nobody else can see.
nobody else believes, nobody else but me."
History
More than a Game

your dreams are yours. they are meant for you, that's why they were placed with you. it is up to you to stay motivated, develop the plan and do the work to make them come alive. don't expect anyone else to understand those dreams of yours. it will only lead to you being discouraged by people that were not meant to understand. dream in color, dream in detail and dream often. how amazing is it to see a picture so clearly when your eyes are closed? have the courage and determination to pursue your dreams and prove to yourself that you have the talent to make them come true. it'll be even more beautiful to see your dreams become real.

i'm living my dreams.

june 11
“ball so hard, this shit weird. we ain't even 'pose to be here. ball so hard, since we here it's only right that we be fair.”
Niggas In Paris
Watch The Throne

sometimes you find yourself in situations that you didn’t sign up for. does that mean that you should give up or do you go for the win? malcolm x famously made a statement about how we didn’t land on plymouth rock. how accurate is that in america? it’s not our game. our ancestors didn’t write the rules, but we go along to get along and as a result, so many of us sit on the sidelines and watch things unfold instead of choosing to actively participate in the process. america is a capitalist society. capitalism is both economic and political, so why do so many of us know so little about economics and politics? get in the game. play hard. even the score. do what you may to re-write the rules.

i will change the game to change the world.

june 12
"when you earnhardt as me eventually you hit a big wall."
Lift Off
Watch The Throne

live in the moment. life is happening now. it's tempting to always be concerned with the future and living for the next moment. this can cause severe anxiety. stop worrying about the future and seize the day. set your intentions for your life and take a step in that direction each day. live every day as if it is your last because it is possible that it may be. what are your plans for today? what are you putting off until tomorrow? how long have your bucket and to-do lists been piling up? start checking things off your list day by day. this will allow you to wake up with a sense of purpose and go to sleep with a sense of accomplishment.

i enjoy the ride.

june 13
"i'm wondering' if a thug's prayers reach."
No Church In The Wild
Watch The Throne

do you sometimes feel as if your prayers are never being answered? do you only talk to god when you want something? how thankful are you for the things that you have? how much time are you spending in meditation? are you prepared for your prayers to be answered? there is a saying that faith without works is dead, so consider the possibility that your faith is being tested because you're not doing the work. how can you expect god to work magic if you are not working yours? begin each day in meditation and end it in prayer. listen before you speak and make sure you're spending the time in between working towards the things that you'd like to see come fruition. do your part, so things can begin to align for you.

i do the work.

june 14
“socrates asks, "whose bias do y'all seek?"”
No Church In The Wild
Watch The Throne

whose approval are you looking for in your life? think about that for a second. now think about why their approval is important you. who are they to judge you? do they exhibit qualities that you hope to one day possess? do they know your story? do you prioritize what others think of you above you choosing to live your life the way you want? do you value their opinion of you more than you value your happiness? you cannot let the praise of others go to your head or their criticisms get to your heart. in this social media age, we seem to place an exaggerated amount of importance on likes and heart emojis. as a result, we also have begun to exaggerate the importance of our opinion about others, even those we don’t know. it is your life; therefore, you have to live with the results of your decisions and actions. don’t live for likes. do what makes you happy and let others do the same.

i am the judge of me.

june 15
"they say a lot about me, let me tell you what i ain't."
Say Hello
American Gangster

everyone has an opinion. people tend to judge others that they know little about based on brief interactions or even based the opinions of others. getting to know people takes time and an open mind. most times you'll find that once you've actually had an opportunity to get to know someone, they're much different than you initially assumed. the best way to find out about a person is to go straight to the source. our experiences influence the people we become, and everyone has a story. no matter what you have been through or done, it is not up to others to judge you. conversely, you are also in no position to judge others no matter what you feel you've accomplished. always remember that the people who matter will never judge you and those that do, don't matter and no one's opinion of you will supersede your own.

i am not defined by other's opinions.

june 16
"i ain't playing', life's short so i aim."
Say Hello
American Gangster

what will your obituary say? what do you want it to say? how do you want people to remember you? what do you want to accomplish? well, stop playing around and get started. don't continue to put things off to the next day, next month, or next year assuming that you have time. set the target, focus and take aim. don't get stuck in a cycle of procrastination, every day take a step in the direction of your goals. how much closer to your dreams would you be if you weren't dragging your feet? stop taking your time for granted. once the moment is lost, you can't get it back. you've got work to do and dreams to fulfill.

i value my time.

june 17
"before i go the world gon feel my pain."
Say Hello
American Gangster

speak your truth. don't try to hide the things that you've been through, even if they may make others uncomfortable. you've survived so much, and all these things have only made you wiser and stronger. be transparent, tell your story. replace the pain of your past with faith for the future. speak up and heal your scars while you make your mark. the world is waiting for all that you have to offer, even if they don't realize it yet. had it not been for everything that you've gone through, you wouldn't be prepared for everything that awaits you. use faith and step into your fate.

i use my pain as fuel for my dreams.

june 18
"cause when my backs against the wall, nigga i react."
Say Hello
American Gangster

out of necessity comes opportunity. sometimes we won't do things until we are forced to. how many times have you waited until the last minute to do something and the outcome was better than you could have imagined? can you even count the times that you've created a way out of no way? you may have learned to cut your hair because you couldn't afford to pay a professional. or you may have learned to sew because you couldn't afford shopping sprees. If you own a business, you may have learned to wear many different hats because you don't currently have the budget for qualified staff. don't ever give up, even when things seem hopeless. get creative. remember that there is no box so you can always figure things out. believe in yourself. you've got this. and remember, that you've always got you.

i won't back down.

june 19
"we get together like a choir, to acquire what we desire."
Can't Knock The Hustle
Reasonable Doubt

teamwork makes the dream work it's true. it's amazing what we can accomplish when we work together. everyone on the team has a position to play if you really expect to win. think about the times you've been a part of a team or had group projects ...what reasons did things work or not work? everyone has to be working toward the same goal. who's on your team? what's everyone's role? what does each person bring to the table? understand that your strengths may be another's weakness and vice versa. while it may be tempting to do things alone in the interest of speed, never forget the power of many. do your part. work together. win together.

i play my part.

june 20
"memories may sneak down my cheek, but i could see a side eye in my sleep."
Caught Their Eyes
4:44

once a relationship or friendship has come to an end and some time has passed, we tend to edit the story to our liking. we gravitate toward the good times, the smiles and laughs and the details of the relationship's downfall become foggy. don't try to convince yourself that someone's repeated bad actions are not a result of bad intentions. people pretend well and there's only so long before their true character reveals itself. everyone won't reciprocate your energy. everyone doesn't value you or what you bring to the table. everyone doesn't believe in authentic, trusting relationships and will try to cut you so you'll never have an opportunity to cut them. never forget and you'll only sharpen your ability to separate friends from foes. going forward, save yourself time and energy as you get better at attracting the real ones. even the people that betray you are a part of the divine plan.

i won't rewrite history.

june 21
"can't complain 'bout what they ain't gon' give ya. that ain't gon' get ya shit, might as well give up."
Say Hello
American Gangster

it's easy to complain about what's wrong and why it's wrong. it takes effort for you to correct the wrongs. always remember that although you may not be responsible for your victimization, you are solely responsible for your own salvation. you cannot expect the person that has victimized you to also be the person that will save you. it's up to you to do for yourself. it's up to you to get back up every single time someone kicks you down. it is your responsibility to get someone's foot off of your own neck. it's unrealistic to expect a bully or a predator to show mercy on you. this is not a fantasy world; this is the real world. don't get caught up on what is and is not fair. don't allow yourself to be defeated. don't throw in the towel. keep swinging. it is up to you whether you sink or swim, never mind who pushed you overboard and who refused to throw you a life jacket.

i am my savior.

june 22
"only god can judge him, only he without sin tell me if my means justified my ends."
Say Hello
American Gangster

it's been said that every saint has a past, and every sinner has a future. so why is that people are so quick to degrade and disregard someone because of their perceived sin. what allows flawed human beings to assign themselves the roll of judge and jury to the actions and decisions other people? how can people who have also sinned criticize the sins of another? it makes them feel less guilty about their own sins. your intuition will guide you as to what is right or wrong. consider the reward of the risks that you take and decide if it's worth it you in the grand scheme of your life. think long term. be sure that you are prepared for the repercussions associated with your choices.

i am judged only by the most high.

june 23
“one out of three of us is locked up doing' time you know what this type of shit can do to a nigga mind?”
Say Hello
American Gangster

how many people do you know that are currently in prison? how many do you know that have ever been to prison? how many do you know that have ever been arrested? what do they all have in common? now, consider the crimes that the people may have committed. do you think they are the only people in america committing those crimes? do you think the punishment fits the crime? the thirteenth amendment to the united states constitution states that slavery is illegal, except in the event of a crime. so, plainly stated, if you are found guilty of a crime, you are now eligible to be enslaved legally. free labor yields high profit margins. don’t believe the hype and don’t get caught up in the mind fucks. open your mind. are you asking the right questions?

i will change the narrative.

june 24
"if you owe me ten dollars you ain't giving' me nine."
Say Hello
American Gangster

have you ever loaned someone money and they never paid you back? have you ever been loaned money to someone, and they are banking on you forgetting about it. get on a payment plan, do what you must, but get it done. someone deemed you trustworthy enough to extend you credit, prove them right if you pay what you owe, you'll always have an advocate that you'll likely be able to reach out to in tough times. who will keep loaning you money if you've already proven yourself to be unreliable? better to stay in the good graces of those to which you are indebted than to make an enemy of someone that once showed you compassion. don't spend your time trying to avoid those that you owe, find ways to pay your debts and be a person of your word. you don't want these things hanging over your head and negatively impacting your reputation.

i pay what i owe and i collect what i'm owed.

june 25
"but there's a price for overdoing it
doing' it this big will put you on the map."
Falling
American Gangster

what do you want to be known for? a pretty face? a nice body? looks fade as we grow older and so will people's memories, unless you're doing it big. how big are your dreams? make sure you're using your talents to gain the success you seek. are you breaking records? are you breaking ceilings? once you've made a name for yourself, how will you use your platform? are you changing lives? are you making history? how big are your goals? aim high. how big are your moves? think hard and work smart. how will you be remembered? are you loved or hated? are you a champ or a chump? all eyes will be on you when you start to make some noise. use the attention of others wisely and make sure you have something to say.

to whom much is given, much is required.

june 26
"can't blow to hard, life's a deck of cards."
Falling
American Gangster

in life we have no control over the hand that is dealt to us, but it is up to us to play the hand we've been dealt. our lives consist of blessings and trials and we have to make the most of them both. we must be grateful for our blessings and in turn, be a blessing to others. we cannot waste time complaining about life's trials and tribulations, but we have to recognize the lessons and apply them. it is up to us whether we let the next card set us back or set us up.

i play my hand to the fullest.

june 27
"before the sun rose, we chasing dollars with a couple of o'z that follow downing bottles of rose'."
Broken English & Drug Sellin'
Demo

the early bird gets the worm. what time do you wake up each morning? are you awakened by a jarring alarm clock that frightens you out of your sleep? do you hit the snooze button repeatedly and never seem to get enough rest? maybe it's not the quality of your sleep, but the quality of your dreams. the chirping of the birds is natures beautiful alarm clock. rise in the morning with the energy to chase your passions. jump out of bed eager to fulfill your destiny and lay a brick each day and each night, toast to a job well-done.

i am eager to live my dreams each day.

june 28
"all this bullshit can make the mind weary but, my theory is the sun shines clearly."
Jay-Z Freestyle
The Professional (DJ Clue)

life can get overwhelming, and it will make you second-guess your faith in the future. that's the thing about faith, it requires that you keep moving forward even if you can't see exactly what's immediately in front you. your belief in what will be, has to be stronger that your fears and anxiety brought on by everything going on in the world. be hopeful about the impact you will have, plant your seeds, water them and be prepared for the sunny days ahead.

i expect sunny days.

june 29
"making sure everybody gets a slice of the pie we dice up."
Feelin' It (Clean)
Reasonable Doubt

when you eat, do you make sure others eat? or do you feast, while others watch? there's enough for everybody. if you divide it fairly you set that expectations that the wealth and opportunities flow freely and fairly. if everyone is eating, you shouldn't have to worry about people's actions as a result of their hunger. allow others an opportunity to thrive. are you protecting yourself, as well as the people that have been involved along the way? treating people unfairly in is a sign of weakness. it indicates that you are worried that a person or group may eventually surpass you if the circumstances were equal. look within. look around you. when have you had opportunities to put people on or share the pie? how did you respond in those situations? did you treat others how they deserved?

life is not fair, but i am.

june 30
"i hope you fools choose to listen i drop jewels bust it. these are the rules i follow in my life you gotta love it."
Feeling It (Edited)

do you have a mentor? a couple of them? who is inspiring you? who is teaching you? who is helping direct you? who is helping redirect you? its great having someone that will allow you to pick their brain. someone that listens to you, and more importantly, someone for you to listen to. someone that will share what they've learned and utilize their relationships and connections to further your agenda. your mentors usually see potential in you that you may not see in yourself. they see everything you are and force you to live up to it. they will help guide you on your path to becoming your best self. they see the possibilities. you won't live long enough to learn all the lessons or make all the mistakes, so learn from someone else's. find someone that understands what you are trying to do. find people that embody qualities that you'd like to see in yourself. open your mind and allow yourself to be enlightened and encouraged.

july 1
"took for my child to be born, to see through a woman's eyes."
4:44
4:44

often, we're insensitive to the plight opposite sex, forgetting that we're all connected. we are all of each other, and on the deepest level we want affection and respect. how would you want your mother or father to be treated? how would you want your son or daughter to be treated? you must remember that everyone is child and most of us will become someone's parent. so often women coddle their sons and create a future fuckboy. and other times, guys seem to only show respect to the women that they're related to. if you put your own shit aside and be considerate, we could avoid being at odds with each other. our family structure might be stronger as a result of us showing empathy for each other instead of carelessness with the hearts and emotions of others.

i will leave people better than i found them.

july 2
"you're a queen you deserve the cream, everything that gleam, everything that shines, everything that's mine."
Anything
The Truth (Beanie Siegel)

women are the creators of life. without women, none of us would be here. that's not up for debate. some people have the attitude that their mother is the most important woman in the world while disrespecting everyone else's mother. hell, some women even disrespect themselves. that's wack and disrespect to one woman is an indication that you might one day disrespect them all. how can you justify tearing down someone that was born with such power? someone that has the ability to bring forth human life. women are to be protected and uplifted so they can raise well-adjusted, balanced and strong children who will one day become the nation's leaders. understand who you are. realize your value. respect your gifts and play your position.

i love and respect women.

july 3
"and if my children knew, i don't even know what i would do."
4:44
4:44

growing up, i'm sure you heard your parents say, "do as i say, not as i do." unfortunately, it doesn't usually work like that. children tend to duplicate their parents' actions. that's why children should serve as motivators to make their parents better people. if you generally have a bad habit of cursing, i'm sure you make an effort to watch your language in the presence of your children. not only do you not want them repeating that behavior, but to some degree you also don't want them looking at you a certain way. children put their parents on a pedestal and consider them to be perfect, not understanding that they too are human. while parents revel in being thought of as superheroes, having children forces you to look in the mirror and reflect on your actions. not only do you not want your children to find out santa claus isn't real, but you also don't want them to think you're not either.

i hold myself accountable.

july 4
“or better yet here's a verse from hamlet "lord, we know who we are, yet we know not what we may be."”
Marcy Me
4:44

have you ever had the feeling that there is something different waiting for you? something better. maybe even something bigger. it’s up to you to find out what that is. what thoughts can you not stop thinking? what excites you? what dreams keep you awake at night? what goals make you jump out of bed in the morning? you know the things that light your fire, so you may as well fuel the flames. you owe it to yourself to set your dreams on fire. you owe it to the people that believe in you and the people that pray for you to fulfill your potential. don’t get discouraged by your fears. don’t be paralyzed by your doubts. don’t allow the critics to get in your head. don’t let the flames die out.

i believe i can fly.

july 5
"so, maybe i'm the one or maybe i'm crazy."
Marcy Me
4:44

if you don't believe in yourself, why should anyone else? you may sometimes feel that you're the only person that believes in you, and that's okay. what is important is that you believe in you. that's all that matters. you are capable. you can do the things you imagine, and no one can do it like you do it. your heart, your head, your talents, your values and your morals all conspire to make everything you do uniquely you. this is your power. you are literally putting your stamp on things that you put out into the world. believe in yourself. believe in your power. there is no one like you, there was no one like you, and there will be no one like you. if that makes you crazy to believe in yourself, embrace being crazy. why would you want to be anything else? you are the most important person in your life. if you believe in you, anything is possible. would you rather believe that you're special and be wrong, our think that you're ordinary and be right?

i am special.

july 6
"came through the bushes smelling like roses i need a trophy just for that."
Marcy Me
4:44

it's not where you come from, its where you're going. you have absolutely no control over how you came into the world and who your parents are or are not. what they have and do not have, what they know and don't know. as a child, you have no control over where you were raised, how much money you have, or how you grow up. what you do have control over, is what you do with it. you can be fueled by your environment and circumstances or you can sit around feeling sorry for yourself. the choice is yours. you are responsible for the outcome, whatever it is, you are in control. remember that, every day when you wake up and are tempted to complain about your past. what will you do with it?

i create my own opportunities.

july 7
“i don't post no threats on the internet
i just pose a threat, blame lenny s. for that.”
Moonlight
4:44

success is the best revenge. have you ever had a disagreement with someone and been tempted to react confrontationally? but what have you compromised and risked in your own life by allowing yourself to be involved in that confrontation? your safety? your livelihood? your character? was it worth it? will it ever be worth it? sometimes, the best thing you can do is remain silent, work hard, and let everything play out. especially in this age of technology. once you put something out in the world, it's almost certainly out there forever to be located by whoever is looking for it. you know what really kills people? seeing someone that they once crossed doing well. especially, if they could've been a part of that success. what's even better, is because you'll be so consumed with the good that's happening in your life, you'll realize how trivial the people that crossed you are. their role in your story is minor. they are non-factors. win with actions, not arguments.

i seek revenge with success.

july 8
"i will not lose, ever."
U Don't Know
The Blueprint

it ain't over 'til it's over and if you aren't where you want to be, then why should you ever concede. things that may be perceived as losses should really be received as lessons if you simply change how you look at each situation. each situation that doesn't go how you'd hoped, should be considered redirection on your road to your dreams and goals. a sore loser is simply someone that fails to recognize the lesson that life is trying to teach them. you can't win all of the little battles in life, but the goal is using the lessons to win the war and create the life that you wish. work hard, be positive, keep your eyes open for opportunities and have a ball.

i'm a winner.

july 9
"i sell ice in the winter, i sell fire in hell. i am a hustler baby i sell water to a well."
U Don't Know
The Blueprint

have you ever gone on a job interview and were asked to sell the pen that the interviewer was holding? did you ever have to sell candy for a fundraiser for a worthy cause? i'm sure you made it happen. you know how to do what you have to, even if it's not easy. expect some nos along the way. use those instances to practice your pitch to get the yes. use what you've got and do what you can to get what you want. what are you good at? where are you from? what are you selling? what problem are you solving? have you ever seen the bucket boys on the corner? how about the dancers on the subway? has a salesman ever walked into your salon or barber shop? find your customer and figure out what they need. tell your story in a way that appeals to them. be focused. be aggressive. be determined. be enthusiastic. go for it and get it done.

i make it happen.

july 10
“i don't be on the 'gram going ham.”
Moonlight
4:44

usually, people only know about you what you share. they have to work with the information given to them or make things up. by most accounts, most people don’t like other people in their business. so, why do so many of us willingly choose to invite people into our lives on social media. do we no longer value our privacy? do we prioritize popularity over privacy? despite all evidence from some of our favorite reality stars that exposure can contribute to the deterioration of relationships, self-esteem and so forth, we still decide to open our lives to strangers. why? why would anyone show the wolves where they lay their head and then let them know when they’re not home? that seems like an obvious invitation to the wrong people to take what’s yours. that goes for your significant others, as well. it’s possible to be the shit without having to publicly shit on anyone. consider what you value and work on protecting your peace and your piece.

i protect what’s important to me.

july 11
“even when we win, we gon' lose”
Moonlight
4:44

as you elevate, you’re going to lose some people that you thought were friends and reveal some enemies you didn’t know you had. your ascension makes them uncomfortable which may result in jealousy, separation and terrorizations. you’ll also find some allies you didn’t know you had. sometimes, we become successful and forget to reach out and reach back. forgetting that a fist is more powerful than a finger. you can’t win the fight without throwing some punches. be clear on who you’re in the ring with, who’s supporting you, who’s cheering you on, who’s tripping you up and who’s rooting against you. align yourself with people working towards impacting the greater good.

when i win, we win.

july 12
"don't follow no nigga, that's hoe shit man. stand on your own two, do yo shit man."
Anything
The Truth (Beanie Siegel)

sheep follow herds. fish swim in schools. wolves move in packs. all of this is intended for protection because there is power in numbers. everyone has a role in the group. there are leaders and there's followers. leading from the rear allows you to see the complete picture and sometimes gives the illusion that you're following. everyone has a role in life. there are predators and there is prey. anyone or anything can become either if you lose sight of the intention behind sticking together and begin to follow blindly without contributing to the decision to move in a particular direction. in every situation, determine if you are leading or following, predator or prey. use your group for protection, not misdirection. be sure that everyone around you is working towards the same goal? use your own legs to follow the direction of your own brain.

i lead.

july 13
“y'all niggas still signing' deals?”
Moonlight
4:44

with all the historic examples we’ve seen of talented people being taken advantage of by greedy industry executives, why do so many of us still look to be validated by those same folks instead of creating our own wave. no one will act in your best interest more than you will. so why not bet on yourself? invest in yourself. you think you’re the shit? prove it. if someone else is willing to make a deal with you, you have to understand that they see your value and your potential. whatever they’re offering you must be a fraction of what you’re worth. it’s up to you to divide the pie in a way that is fair to you. it is up to you to get up every day and play your hand. don’t be so thirsty that you drink from their poisonous cup. don’t allow yourself to become prey to a predator and put your destiny in someone else’s hands.

i believe in my own abilities.

july 14
"fuck what we selling. fuck is we making?"
Moonlight
4:44

how many people do you know with a t-shirt line? a restaurant? a barbershop? a salon? those are all solid efforts at entrepreneurship. conversely, how many people do you know with clothing factories? beauty products companies or distribution facilities? grocery stores? farms? if you're not supplying the product at its source, you're only a customer and without that supply, you know longer have a business. the goal is to own and control. if you own a restaurant, your friend should own the grocery store and his uncles should own the farm. what are you making?

i provide the wave.

july 15
"cause they grass is greener cause they always raking in more."
Moonlight
4:44

so often we try to replicate the outcome of things without replicating the process. we want to look rich without doing the work to accumulate the wealth. we want to be skinny without working out or eating right. we want happiness without working on ourselves and while still choosing to engage in things that we know make us unhappy. cut the bullshit, then use it to fertilize your soil. do the work every day and you'll begin to see the fruits of your labor. you can't get the same outcome without putting in the same work.

i nurture the things i want and expect to grow.

july 16
"sometimes you need your ego, gotta remind these fools."
Bam
4:44

humbling yourself generally requires getting rid of your ego. however, ego is synonymous with self-esteem and self-respect. why would you ever want to remove those things? there is a difference between having ego and being egotistical. being egotistical is having inflated self-esteem and self-importance. there is nothing wrong with believing in yourself and honoring yourself. in fact, its mandatory. it sets the tone for others to be clear of what you demand of them. know yourself, know your worth and respectfully make sure that others know it as well and make sure they will never forget.

i know my worth.

july 17
“y'all be talking' crazy under them ig pictures.”
Bam
4:44

social media was created to allow us an opportunity to be more sociable. to spread the love and the news. to allow others a snapshot at our real lives. to serve as a sort of time capsule for our lives. so, why do so many people flex for the gram and spread hate, lies and irrelevance. instead of using social mediums for the good that they're capable of we'd rather flex on each other and incriminate ourselves. if you were at an interview and they pulled up your social media, would they hire you? what about a date? for some reason in front of a judge? would you be friends with you? if you answered no, that may be why you don't get callbacks from jobs or dates. is your tone a little too aggressive? a little too conceited? are your posts reflective of your reality? look in the mirror and think about what type of energy and information you're putting into the world and onto others newsfeed. would you hang with you? spread love on your feed and in life.

i trust actions over captions.

july 18
“my advice is just don't be too nice to niggas. set the price on niggas and live your live, my nigga.”
Bam
4:44

the wrong people will take your kindness and understanding for weakness if you allow them. are you clear of your boundaries? are you clear with others about them? do you constantly let people cross the line that you’ve drawn with no repercussions? stop letting shit slide. don’t allow your acceptance of people’s actions to devalue and disrespect you. don’t intentionally do anyone harm, but don’t take any shit either. if you’re not clear, you will continuously be violated by line-crossers. this could be friends, family, acquaintances, clients, business partners and more. draw your lines, set your price.

i am clear on my boundaries.

july 19
"nothing wrong with the aim, gotta change the target."
American Dreamin'
American Gangster

if you know how to sell girl scout cookies, you can sell cars. don't allow yourself to be put in a box and more importantly, don't put yourself in that box. think big. dream big. do the work. the opportunities are endless. believe in yourself. don't continue to question if you're capable and talk yourself out of what's possible. you've got this. work towards goals where the rewards are worth the risks. challenge yourself to do something different, something better, something more rewarding. be fueled by your confidence in yourself and level up.

my skills are transferable.

july 20
“take those moneys and spread 'cross families.”
Legacy
4:44

are you working collectively with others in your family to build wealth, businesses and overall strengthen the legacy of your family? are you educating your family about saving, investing and entrepreneurship? work on providing stability, employment opportunities and financial security for your family and develop a plan that will allow the fruits of your labor to pass the baton to the next generation and so forth. think about the trumps, the hiltons and the rockefellers. no matter what your personal feelings about the families are, facts are facts. what will your family be known for in 100 years?

i am building a dynasty.

july 21
"i'd like to see, a nice peace-fund ideas from people who look like we."
Legacy
4:44

do you support programs that help people from the community you came from? do you mentor kids from your old school? are you taking advantage of your company's matching gifts program to contribute to the charities of your choice? are you doing your part to give back to worthy causes and cultivate the change that you'd like to see in the world? be clear, you don't have to carry the world on your shoulders. but it is up to you to act and do your part. don't sit back in helplessness, just do something. are you feeding the hungry? educating the ignorant? supporting local small businesses? helping create jobs? don't allow yourself to get overwhelmed. take a look around and take note of where your community is suffering and do whatever you can to help, even if you think its small. every little bit counts and adds up if we're all doing something.

i give back to my community.

july 22
“we gon' start a society within society.
that's major, just like the negro league.”
Legacy
4:44

when people say you can’t sit with them, sometimes it’s best to build your own table. what you create will be more reflective of your best interests and your values anyway instead of having to fit in to a group that may have only allowed you in by force. don’t surround yourself with people that merely tolerate you. ask yourself why you want to be a part of that circle. you may find that it may be your stubbornness simply wanting what you think you can’t have, despite that group not actually being what you need or even genuinely want. how are you being improved by that group? who’s benefiting from your presence? who’s suffering from your absence?

i surround myself with likeminded people.

july 23
i've been listening to wu-tang and niggas like "your seed, married his seed, married my seed"
that's how we keep carter money all in the family."
Legacy
4:44

throughout your years of dating how many times have you encountered people that don't share your values, morals, manners or ways of thinking. i'm sure you've been absolutely baffled and appalled at the differences. there's no way you can build anything of value with someone with different values. that's usually why we are able to form strong bonds in our friendships, because of these shared ideals. so why is it when we start to have our own families, we allow the change in our life to create distance in our friendships instead of solidifying your village? what is clear is that they will raise children with similar values. does it make sense to send your children out into the world to one day date and marry people that have conflicting values and potentially dismantle what you've spent your life building instead of adding to it.

i set my children up for success from the start.

july 24
“i was running from him; he was giving me wisdom.”
Legacy
4:44

how much time do you spend with your grandparents, uncles and aunts? do you listen to their stories? do you ask them questions? or do you just tune out when they start to talk about their experiences? if you listen closely, you may find the lessons in their life, the world and people in those stories. you may even get some insight into yourself. pay attention. tuning in could possibly help you avoid lots of mistakes or connect the dots. did it ever occur to you that these people may have learned some things in the decades that they’ve been on this earth? think about all the things you learned in your time here. now multiply that. there is nothing new under the sun, so it’s highly likely that they have seen most of things you’re going through or will go through in another form and at another time. you can avoid lots of mistakes is you learn from the mistakes of others.

i seek knowledge and lesson from my elders.

july 25
“see how the universe works? it takes my hurt and help me find more of myself. it's a gift and a curse.”
Legacy
4:44

do you allow the things that hurt you to make you bitter or better? if you take a break from crying and reflect on the things and people that have hurt you, you’ll find that these are opportunities to make you a better person. stop being the victim. emerge victorious from the bullshit. if you allow people that have hurt you to harden you, then they’ve won. remember that hurt people hurt people. sometimes, people hurt others without even realizing it or without knowing why. dig deep and get to the bottom of that, be sympathetic as to why and work on figuring out how this hurdle is setting you up for the win. if you can put yourself back together again, you’ll find that you’re even better than you were before. those hurts allow you to be more sympathetic to others, more insightful and become a better person overall. allow these situations to build you instead of breaking you.

i understand the lessons that life has taught me.

july 26
"you run this hard just to stay in place. keep up the pace, baby, keep up the pace."
Legacy
4:44

do you hate mondays? does wednesday seem like you worked a whole week already? does the weekend not seem long enough? does the job you work literally make time stand still? when you get paid, how quickly do you spend the money that you worked so hard to earn? what are you spending it on? was it worth those terrible mondays and the short weekends? are you doing something with your money that will buy you time later? will your days off eventually become longer than those excruciating workdays? are you making progress with your earnings? are you providing yourself and your family some security, so you don't feel like you're on a treadmill? out a breath and exhausted and seemingly not going anywhere. reexamine what you're doing and make sure you're making moves that make sense.

i make moves towards progress.

july 27
"confidence you exude make the fools stay away."
713
EVERYTHING IS LOVE

do you have friends that always seem to be involved in drama? with the people they date. with other friends? with their co-workers? with their family? or maybe you're the one that's always in shit. first, check yourself. what are you doing that encouraging the bullshit? are you the one that's instigating the issues? if so, knock it off. if not, maybe it's your energy. what are you inviting into your life? trust, when you make it clear that you won't tolerate the bullshit with what you choose to entertain, people that are on bullshit will stay far away from you. make a habit of shutting down things that bring you down and eventually you won't even have to shut it down, it won't even come your way. you may wonder why some people don't hit you up or try to connect with you ... it's because they know you're not on what they're on ... and that's a good thing.

my good energy keeps away bad intentions.

july 28
"we only know love because of ya. america's a muthafucka to us, lock us up, shoot us. shoot our self-esteem down, we don't deserve true love."
713
EVERYTHING IS LOVE

this world will chew you up and spit you out. sometimes we get so absorbed in how the world is abusing us that we don't consider how we may be abusing others. we add to that abuse instead of being a force of good vibes, source of comfort or a voice of compassion, an encourager or a lover. with women, sometimes the only man that we speak softly to is our son. with men, sometimes the only woman they'll only uplift is their mother. Forgetting that everyone is someone's daughter or son and most of us will eventually be someone's mother or father. if you wouldn't want someone talking to or treating your son or daughter a particular way, don't be the cause of that treatment for someone else's child and don't be the recipient of it, either. treat people with love and respect. we're all fighting battles that we may not share with the world. make each other better and help heal each other's hurts.

i respect women and men as creators of life.

july 29
“tight circle, no squares, i'm geometrically opposed to you”
FRIENDS
EVERYTHING IS LOVE

squares box you in. they limit your potential and try to lock you in to their borders. circles are free flowing and keep it moving. surround yourself with people that keep the energy, ideas, support, encouragement and money flowing. who’s in your circle? do they encourage your growth, or do they instigate your bullshit? do you feel confined? do they lock you into their ideas of who you should be? do you feel confined and limited? if so, that’s not a friendship bracelet, that’s a handcuff. break free! don’t allow yourself to be boxed in by small minds. those aren’t your people. find a new tribe. make sure you’re a part of the right circle

i know that the world is round & prison is a box.

july 30
"they even biting cornrows, put your scarecrows up. i come from the finest crop."
BLACK EFFECT
EVERYTHING IS LOVE

the things that make you are so much a part of you that you sometimes take them for granted. have you ever been complimented on something, maybe your shape or your skin, and you're so used to yourself that you don't see anything special about it? all the while, someone's at home using makeup to copy your nose shape, or with a cabinet full of products to get your hair texture or paying cosmetic surgeons to get the body that you inherited from the women in your dad's family. don't take the things that make up you for granted. embrace them. be grateful. celebrate them. learn how to make the things that your grandma made for sunday dinner, restaurants are making millions selling collard greens and fried chicken with a side of watermelon. if you don't claim what's yours, you'll leave it to be claimed by someone else who sees the value in it, even if they once acted like they didn't. have you ever lost something at a lost & found? what happens if you don't claim it? the same goes for your culture.

i celebrate my ancestry and culture.

july 31
"when i say, "free the dogs," i free 'em, that's how meek got his freedom."
FRIENDS
EVERYTHING IS LOVE

do you have friends or family that are incarcerated? if you do, you probably feel like you're doing time with them to some degree. with the high costs of collect phone calls, books, full day road trips for short visits, contributions to commissary, it can be overwhelming. not to mention the time and effort and emotional investment to write letters and communicate with attorneys. i once read a story about a woman who went to law school so she could become an attorney to appeal her brother's life sentence. it worked. how hard do you go? do you lobby to change legislation? do you pay lawyer's fees? do you make visits? do you send your loved ones books to open their minds and keep their spirit alive? did you encourage them to seek out other paths to avoid their current predicament? when you say "free the guys" is it just a sound bite or are you working on ways to free the guys?

i walk it like i talk it.

august 1
"you got niggas in the feds, you ain't even tryna feed em."
FRIENDS
EVERYTHING IS LOVE

free the guys. your fathers, brothers, sons, uncles, cousins, friends. free their bodies and more importantly, free their minds. send them books, send some money, find an attorney, do what you can. understand that nobody's free until we're all free. don't talk about it, be about it. if anyone is enslaved, it is proof that it is possible to do it to others and as things advance that bondage is likely to follow. in accordance with the 13th amendment of the united states constitution imprisonment is, in fact, slavery. read it in full. brainstorm ways to free them, but even further brainstorm and execute ways to help them to avoid the trap.

i will free the guys.

august 2
"don't listen to your crew, do what works for you."
Anything
The Truth (Beanie Siegel)

peer pressure is real. sometimes you can be pressured by your peers without even realizing it. you just call it friendship. if you only drink or smoke when you're with your friends, it might be peer pressure. if you don't like someone because your friend didn't like them back in fourth grade and you've never even had a conversation with the person, it might be peer pressure. you don't support a business because your friend complained about them, but your experience was positive. you quit your job because your friend quit. you don't go on vacation because your friend didn't go. you're out partying with your friends every night, even though you had work to do. pay attention. show some strength. make your own decisions about who to befriend, where to go and what to think and do. don't allow people to use friendship as a justification to lead you down the wrong path.

i do what works for me.

august 3
"i ain't going' to nobody nothing' when me and my wife beefing."
FRIENDS
EVERYTHING IS LOVE

what are your priorities? family? success? good health? attaining wealth? does what you say your priorities are align with your actions? do you put partying above working? do you put spending ahead of earning? do you put your indulgences above your health? now, answer the question regarding your priorities based on your actions. are you taking care of your business? are you taking care of your family? are you taking care of yourself? or are you distracted? we need to be clear on what our priorities are and be sure that our actions are reflecting those. you may upset some people with your decisions since your priorities may not be the same as theirs. but this is your life, and you have to be sure that you're doing what you need to do to have balance in your life.

i prioritize my family.

august 4
"i come from the finest crop."
BLACK EFFECT
EVERYTHING IS LOVE

have you ever lost something that belonged to you and were lucky enough to be able to claim it in the lost and found? what if you arrived to claim your item and someone else was claiming that it was theirs? would you fight for what's yours or would you just release it to the new owner? what if the person that was trying to claim it had previously mocked you for owning the item? how would you feel? what would you do? sometimes we take for granted the things that contributed to our cultivation. the communities we grew up in. the music we grew up on. the television shows we watched. the food we ate. our physical features. these things are engrained in us and we're so used to them that we don't think much of them. when in fact, this is our culture. it is who we are. it is to be celebrated, not forgotten. each time you celebrate who you are it is a reminder to everyone who the rightful owner is and an understanding that nobody does it better than the originator.

i celebrate who i am and where i'm from.

august 5
"to get her back, i had to sweat her. **y'all could make up with a bag, i had to change the weather."**
LOVEHAPPY
Everything is Love

has anyone ever disrespected you publicly and tried to apologize to you privately? have you ever wronged someone and tried to move past it without addressing how you can make it right? we're all capable of making mistakes, none of us are perfect. keep in mind that mistakes can be costly. your actions to rectify the situation reflect your acceptance of your wrong and the seriousness of your willingness to correct it. the gravity of your apology is indicative of how much you value that person and your relationship with that person. however, it isn't required that the victim of your offense accept your apology. but your apology is not about their acceptance, it is about your admittance to your wrongdoing. let go of your pride and take the necessary steps to correct your wrongs to those that are important to you.

the magnitude of my apologies matches the offense.

august 6

"take your time when you're liking a guy. cause if he senses that your feelings to intense, its pimp or die."
Song Cry
The Blueprint

have you ever met someone that you really connected with and you immediately wanted to make them apart of your everyday life? has anyone ever done that to you? how'd it feel? generally, we are being relentlessly pursued by others, our instinct is to run! or, when we allow them to catch us without much pursuit, they don't assign much value to us because they didn't put a lot of effort into getting it. but when the feelings are mutual, you actually have time to learn about the person and determine if the person that you once found so intriguing, is as great as you thought they were and if they think you're as great as they first made you feel. time reveals things about people. this way, you can minimize the risks of being fooled or abused. be patient and enjoy the process and know when to excuse yourself.

i enjoy the process of getting to know people.

august 7
"fake news y'all choose, we no lie no photoshop, just real life."
LOVEHAPPY
EVERYTHING IS LOVE

do you do your research? or do you just accept the things that are presented to you without considering the source? what do they have to gain by telling you certain things? what do you have to lose by accepting those things? in the age of internet search engines, there is no need to be left in the dark and choose to remain ignorant. in the time that it takes to scroll a social media feed you can google a story from an unbiased news source. in the time that it takes to edit and post a photograph, you can read that story. there is no excuse for not knowing. it is a choice. a choice not to pursue the information. a choice not to dig for jewels. a choice to ignore the facts and what's real because a lie is more attractive. what do you choose?

i can handle the truth.

august 8
"i said no to the super bowl, you need me, i don't need you."
APEST**
EVERYTHING IS LOVE

do you know your worth? what do you bring to the table? do you understand the value you add to other people, to brands, to politicians, to businesses? what is your role? do you play your position, or do you go along to get along? you have to, first, understand the value that you bring and leverage that to get the outcome you deem proper. i'm sure you've heard the saying that if you don't stand for something, you'll fall for anything. what do you stand for? what values do you uphold that are enough to make you withdraw your participation or change your vote to get the outcome you desire? is there anything? what do you stand for?

i stand for what's right.

august 9
"niggas getting jerked, that shit hurts, i take it personally."
BOSS
EVERYTHING IS LOVE

have you ever witnessed someone being taken advantage of, disrespected or bullied by another? how'd you respond? was your thought that it wasn't you, so why should you care? you know why? because if they'll do it to someone else, they'll do it to you ... if you let them. you're watching them do it to someone else can be interpreted as condoning the behavior. sucker shit is sucker shit, no matter who the victim is. don't get so comfortable to think someone of sketch character won't be sketchy with you. you just might be at the back of the line of the people they'll do it to. when it's your turn, it's your turn.

i recognize if they do it to you, they'll try to do it to me.

august 10
"niggas rather work for the man than to work with me."
BOSS
EVERYTHING IS LOVE

if you spent your career selling cars and a friend or acquaintance of yours had the initiative to open their own dealership, would you go work with them or would you choose to work for their competitor? if you were in the market to buy a car, who would you shop with? honestly. would you be slightly jealous that you didn't open a dealership? would you find all sorts of criticisms of them, their work ethic and their business to rationalize not working with them? conversely, would you refer your network to them and offer them constructive insight to help them thrive? be honest with yourself about whether you're a hater and if your preventing progress by refusing to work cooperatively. don't only work with folks when you don't have any other options. or be happy for others because you have an ulterior motive. make sure your actions are helping build and not tearing down.

i am a part of the solution.

august 11
"pride always goeth before the fall."
BOSS
EVERYTHING IS LOVE

would you rather lose a person you care about, an opportunity you hoped for or your pride? grow up. don't be so stubborn that you refuse to apologize, forgive or ask for assistance. pride can be a destructive trait if it's not used properly. it can you everything and leave you with nothing, all because of your egotistical ways. when you've wronged someone, ask for forgiveness. when you need help, ask for assistance. when you don't know something, ask for information. it's better to ask early than to do so forcibly. focus on your growth and trust in the compassion and forgiveness of others.

i am humble.

august 12
"i'm different. can't base what i'm gon' be off of what everybody isn't."
So Ambitious
The Blueprint 3

your power is in you being exactly who you are. have confidence in who you are and understand that confidence has no competition. why would you want to be anyone else? it is likely their confidence in who they are that has drawn you to them. you might think it's the clothes, talent or whatever. but understand, it is the confidence. there are lots of beautiful, talented, wealthy people that go unnoticed every day because they lack confidence. believe in yourself. know who you are. you are an original. you were not put here to be like everyone else. you're to a clone. you're real. you're different. show the world the real you. show the world what's great about you.

i play to my strengths.

august 13
“everybody's bosses 'til it's time to pay for the office. ‘til them invoices, separate the men from the boys, over here.”
BOSS
EVERYTHING IS LOVE

today’s music and the current culture has everyone claiming to be a boss. even people that have never once hired, fired or interviewed anyone else have proclaimed themselves bosses. why? what have they done? this is another instance of people wanting the glamour associated with a position without putting in the work to manifest that position. do you even want to be a boss? do you want that responsibility? lots of people depend on real bosses to properly strategize and delegate tasks to keep the lights on and feed their families. can you handle it? there’s nothing wrong with playing your position. do your part and focus on what you’re good at. in order to be an effective leader, you must have a loyal following. there’s nothing worse than a boss that doesn’t pay the bills.

i play my position.

august 14
"we measure success by how many people successful next to you."
BOSS
EVERYTHING IS LOVE

the idea of being self-made is an illusion. while you may have the talent and done the work, you didn't do it alone. there were others around who helped your dream come to life. who's on your team? what's their role? are they putting in work? how are they being rewarded? are you reciprocating their investment in your dream by reinvesting in theirs? if you're selfish enough to only think about yourself and not put others in a position to win also, you need to take a hard look in the mirror. why wouldn't you want them to shine also? do you require all of the attention? are you the only one that can be in the spotlight do you think their success will detract from yours? actually, it will add to. its only lonely at the top if you keep your foot on other people's necks.

i share the wealth.

august 15
"here we say you broke if everybody else broke except for you."
BOSS
EVERYTHING IS LOVE

do you always have to pay the bill? why? are you surrounded by people that are not on your level financially? why is that? does it make you feel good to be the big fish in the small pond? or do they lack motivation, hustle or even money management skills? figure out the problem and correct it. is it you or is it them? if these are people you want in your life it must be corrected. either you'll end up like mc hammer because you're content with feeding them instead of teaching them how to fish. or you'll end up on the menu because of your need to be the big fish. share the knowledge and the resources in order to create opportunities for your team to provide for themselves and their families. being the only one with fat pockets ultimately won't work in your favor, because if you're the only one eating, eventually they'll eat you.

i teach others how to fish.

august 16
"my great-great-grandchildren already rich."
BOSS
EVERYTHING IS LOVE

how big are your goals? how big are your moves? how many generations of people with your last name will benefit from the things you accomplish in your lifetime? how about the seeds you plant? not just financial investments, but information. if you were the first in your family to have life insurance, make sure your children's children own the agency. if you were the first to go to college, see to it that the next generation doesn't need to take out a loan. if you were miseducated, make sure that the information is not hidden from your children. do you part to make up for lost ground and correct the missteps, misdeeds and misinformation of the past that adversely impacted the path for your family. make sure that no one else in your family has to be victim to the things you were exposed to again take control and take the steps to ensure that the bullshit stops with you.

i plant the seeds for my family tree.

august 17
"what would you do, you knew you couldn't fail."
NICE
EVERYTHING IS LOVE

what do you dream about? what do you hope for? do you want a be a millionaire? do you wish you could fly? do you want to go to the moon? what's stopping you? your mind? the opinions of others? your fear of failure? now, let's assume your mind is wide open, others' opinions of you don't matter and as long as you keep trying you are guaranteed a win ... what would you set out to do? dream big. plan big. act big. do it real big. this life is yours and you owe it to yourself to try all of things that interest you. all of the things that you wish for. don't wait until it's too late and you're sitting around saying i wish i would've, could've, should've. just do it. there are people far less qualified than you living your dreams because they did not let fear get in their way.

i will face my fears and live my dreams.

august 18
‘i have no fear of anything, do everything well.”
NICE
EVERYTHING IS LOVE

i’m sure there are things that you claim to not be good at. ask yourself, how hard have you tried? really? most things are muscle memory. you become better with practice. if you can’t cook, keep trying, watch cooking shows, take cooking lessons and watch how you improve with consistent practice. if you’re not good at mathematics, relax. keep counting. keep studying. your limits are only in your mind. you can’t give things a half-hearted effort and expect to perform like the best in the game. you get out of things what you put into them.

i put my heart in everything i do.

august 19
“i have no fear of death, we all born to do that.”
NICE
EVERYTHING IS LOVE

the only thing we’re guaranteed in this life is it will eventually come to an end. it will definitely come for all of us. we may not know how ow when, but we do know that it will come. so why do we waste the time that we do have worrying about the inevitable? if we enjoy being alive so much, then why do we allow ourselves to be distracted from the experience. live in each moment you’re allowed. enjoy your friends and family. help others. learn as much as you can. experience as much as you can. make sure your life is worth living and you’re not just biding your time.

august 20
"last name 'gon be here forever."
NICE
EVERYTHING IS LOVE

i'm sure you've heard of the rockefellers and the waltons. hell, you might even be keeping up with the kardashians. what do these families have in common? one of the family members took a risk and used their hard work to create opportunities for their family for generations to come. who do you put on for? what are doing to make sure that your family leaves an imprint on the world? what type of action are you encouraging? what type of business are you starting? will the people in your family remain relatively unknown or will they make a difference in the world that all started with you? every day is an opportunity to make history. with what you do, who you raise and what you change. what are you doing?

i am making history.

august 21
"i'm clear why i'm here, how about you?"
Family Feud
4:44

what is your purpose? how will you be remembered? will you be remembered? what are you doing to ensure that you will be? how will others tell the story of you? will it be a bunch of half-naked, gym and mirror pics of your outfits? or will people remember you for how you've changed lives and changed the world? for how you made people feel? for the impact you had on the world. what school did you go to? who was it named for? what did they do? wouldn't you like to have your own school? who's your favorite musician? who's on the money you carry every day? figure out what you're passionate about and get busy using that passion to leave your mark.

i live a life of purpose.

august 22
"you'd rather be old rich me or new you?"
Family Feud
4:44

who are you inspired by? whose life would you like to have? understand that you can't have their life, but you can certainly create your own and customize it to your liking with things exactly as you'd like them. why would you want to live someone else's dream? that sounds like a nightmare. you can certainly use the lives of others to give you some insight into the things you'd like to see in your life, and maybe even some things you can live without. our dreams usually reflect our best selves in the best circumstances. live your life. go after the things you want for you instead of aspiring to be someone else. your potential is limitless if you put in work. no one is better than you. the difference between you and them is that their dreaming big and acting on those dreams. be the you of your dreams.

i am my highest self.

august 23
"what's better than one billionaire? two."
Family Feud
4:44

there is power in numbers. while it is great accomplishment for you to have achieved success and wealth, wouldn't it be greater if the people around you were able to do the same? or are you content with being the only accomplished one? or shall i say the only crab to make it out of the barrel. unfortunately, a lot of people have this mindset. it's time to turn that on its head. matter of fact, it's time to flip the barrel over and free everyone. if everyone has achieved some success, we can all be of assistance to each other during life's tough times. things look pretty bleak if only one person has the means to help everyone. if that person falls, there is no one to catch them. allow everyone the freedom to pursue their goals and the opportunity to shine. right now, it's dark, but as each of us fulfills our potential, we'll start to light up stars in the sky.

i am my brother's keeper.

august 24
"i'll fuck up a good thing if you let me."
Family Feud
4:44

people can only do to you what you allow and vice versa. you cannot expect your victimizer to also be your salvation. it is up to you to be your own savior. you have to set boundaries about what you will and will not tolerate and stand firm. be prepared to respond however the situation demands to ensure that you are no longer subjected to their bullshit. don't keep begging for change and redrawing the line expecting a disrespectful person to respect you. it is your job to demand respect. your failure to enforce your expectations of their behavior shows a lack of respect for self. and if you aren't even respecting yourself, why should they? regardless of how good your intentions are toward them or how good the possibilities may be, you have to look at the situation for what is.

i respect boundaries.

august 25
"more than ever we gon have to stick together."
Blue's Freestyle / We Family
4:44

i'm sure you've heard of the good ole' days. the days when people had each other's backs, not stabbed them in it. when neighbors looked out for each other from the safety of their homes to the safety of their children not robbed them of them. the days when people instinctually supported those that shared their struggle, not try to tear them down. so, what happened? somehow, we allowed ourselves to divide, and our concept of community and togetherness was annihilated. and where has that gotten us? seemingly, we've regressed from the progress we'd struggled to make. it's like we're running on a treadmill. link up. be clear on what things are weakening your position. connect with your friends, family and network and discuss what synergies you may have to build your vision. how can you become stronger and advance towards progress instead of allowing yourselves to perish?

i support a larger vision.

august 26
"broken is better than new,
that's kintsukuroi."
MaNyfaCedGod
4:44

kintsugi is the japanese art of repairing broken pottery with gold, silver, or platinum embraces flaws. any damage done is seen as important to the piece's history, rather than something needing to be thrown-away or disguised. don't fake a perfect life. keep it real. the things you've been through contribute to your character and make you who you are. it's all about perspective, and you must understand that it's your so-called imperfections that make you perfectly you. these flaws and scars all have a story. your story. let your scars be reminders to you of what you've survived and the lessons you've learned as a result that have helped correct your direction. your flaws can't be used against you if you embrace them.

i accept my flaws.

august 27
“it’s getting too late we can’t afford mistakes.”
MaNyfaCedGod
4:44

to make a mistake is to be human. the only way to avoid them altogether is by sitting still and doing absolutely nothing. unfortunately, this way you have absolutely no change of doing anything right either. each mistake you make is an opportunity to learn a valuable lesson. for instance, if you had to learn the hard way that there’s a speed monitoring camera on a street, i’m sure you’ll drive cautiously the next time. what have you learned for your mistakes? if you are not learning, then what are you doing? you’re doomed to repeat the missteps you’ve made in the past if you’re not taking note of the lessons. use your lessons from the past to avoid repeating the same mistakes, and you also could benefit from learning from the mistakes of others. turn those mistakes into milestones on your journey. use those lesson to allow you to more clearly see the path towards the realization of your vision. don’t waste any more time repeating mistakes from your past.

i learn from my mistakes.

august 28
“our external reality is an opportunity to heal our internal upset.”
MaNyfaCedGod
4:44

life happens and in our early years what happens to us is generally beyond our control. however, it is those things that create the person we have become. as we grow older, we realize that it is up to us to create the life that we want and become the person we hope to be. regardless of our past, we are in control of our perspective of our present circumstances and what becomes of our future. are you clinging to your past hurts, mistakes and circumstances? let go of the things that you didn’t choose and make choices to allow yourself to become who you really are. everything you encounter in life is either a guide toward your future or a reflection of your past. figure out which is which and handle it accordingly. everyone you meet has something to teach you. the people that hurt you and love you all play a part in helping you become who you’re meant to be. take advantage.

i am healed by the world.

august 29
"standing back from situations, gives you the perfect view. see the snakes in the grass and wait on they ass."
Anything
The Truth (Beanie Siegel)

stop jumping to conclusions. things aren't always what they seem at first glance. what you thought was a snake might actually be a water hose and vice versa. stand back to allow yourself the space to respond appropriately. assess the situation with a clear mind. use your intuition, reference your lessons from the pass and trust yourself first. patience is a virtue and time reveals all, so if you separate your emotions from the situation and allow yourself to look at a situation logically, you'll increase the likelihood of making the best move.

i think logically.

august 30
"love is a battlefield; we all get scars."
You're Welcome Feat Mary J. Blige

i'm sure you've heard the saying that all is fair in love and war. sometimes the line between the two is so blurred that you may not know which is which. love demands that you allow yourself to be vulnerable to your loved one and you trust them to love you despite your flaws and past hurts and elevate you in a way you have yet to experience, and you are expected to do the same for them. that vulnerability can cause you to experience the highest highs and sometimes, the lowest lows. we're all a sum of our experiences, both good and bad, and that paired with our humanness that guarantees that we will sometimes make mistakes and take the people we love for granted at some point can guarantee that we will eventually hurt the person we love or be hurt by the person that person. this reality is what causes so many people to be guarded in their love relationships and in some cases can be the thing that will cause them to hurt the next person. you'll win some and you'll lose some. but you'll live to see another day. allow your scars to heal.

i show love daily.

august 31
"people going thru pain, i'm just talking em thru it."
You're Welcome Feat Mary J. Blige

sometimes when you feel that you are broken you are having a breakthrough. it can help to find a friend, family member or professional to hear, hold and heal your pain. sometimes you just need someone to listen to you vent and allow you an opportunity to get some things off your chest. other times you may need a fresh set of eyes and ears about your experiences to offer you a different perspective. other times you need someone to probe and dig into the situation to help you understand your real feelings. take control of your life, work out the kinks and find healthy ways to make the necessary changes to help you heal your wounds. life can hurt sometimes but stay hopeful about the future and how you'll look back one day and see how far you've come. just take it one day at a time.

i get better every day.

september 1
"i taught you how to fish and not let other niggas feed you. you're welcome."
You're Welcome Feat Mary J. Blige

if you were fired from your job today, how long could you feed yourself? do you have a garden? how long would you have a roof over your head? do you own your home? how long would you have transportation? is your vehicle paid for? how long could you survive? do you have savings? investments? do you have a means to make money that doesn't involve relying on payday? who do you rely on to feed you? you are always at the mercy of whoever controls your food supply. that's why dogs are so loyal. who has you at their mercy?

i depend on me.

september 2
"all that nickel and dime shit don't hold no weight."
Only A Customer
Streets is watching

baby steps count on your journey, but only if you keep moving. ultimately, you will have gained ground over time. your leap of faith will one day produce the results of a giant leap. don't allow yourself to become arrogant as a result of your small wins. some people like to celebrate every shot made in a big way instead of remaining focused on winning the championship. remember, the game ain't over 'til it's over, so while the pints add up, it's the final score that matters.

i go big or go home.

september 3
“it's all good cause the streets is a&r'ing this.”
So Ambitious
The Blueprint 3

why do we look for the validation of the general market? we set the trends. we make things popular that translate into popular culture. jordan sneakers that we wore over 25 years ago are more popular than ever now. did we capitalize on that? use this as a valuable lesson. why not use that power of controlling the tide to make our own products popular with the general market? you set the standard and the rest of the world will follow. don’t believe me? do your research.

i use my power wisely.

september 4
"i know the difference between a bitch and a bey."
I Need Love. (Freestyle)

everyone you date won't be the person that you'll spend the rest of your life with. however, you can best believe that your relationship with them will teach you both something. even if it's what you don't want in a mate. you and the other person will influence each other, and you may pick up things from this relationship that you will want to carry into future relationships and other things, you may leave behind. they might introduce you to a great date night spot or make it easier for you to spot certain characteristics. treat people with respect always but know who to put on a pedestal.

i know who i'm dealing with.

september 5
“men lie women lie, numbers don't.”
Reminder
The Blueprint 3

people are tricky. things usually aren’t black and white. you may sometimes get overwhelmed with having to read between the lines and decipher what people have said in order to understand what they really mean. you may have heard someone say “i don’t care” but they can’t stop talking about the subject. or the guy you’re dating may be lying about his situation and what you’re observing isn’t adding up. but the numbers should always add up. the amount of time that you spend on something should reflect its importance to you. the amount of effort put into something should reflect the outcome. the number of calories you consume, and burn will be reflected in your weight. the dollars that you invest should reflect the return. if the numbers aren’t adding up, make some adjustments. its simple mathematics.

i know that math is much simpler than people.

september 6
"do you already, enough of the complaining boo-who's already."
Already Home
The Blueprint 3

no one can do you like you and everyone won't understand you. those that don't understand may not be meant to. instead of devoting effort and energy to acknowledging your haters and complaining about what you could be doing and those who have chosen to reject you or your talents, redirect that energy into working on your craft and improving yourself. do you. make things happen for yourself. if you want to lose weight, do it. if you hate your job, update your resume and start searching for a new one. if you feel like your friends aren't holding you down, work on being the kind of friend you deserve. don't waste precious time complaining. nothing will come from it. you're responsible for changing your predicament. if you're not bothered enough to do the work and make a change, then save the complaining.

i'm doing me.

september 7
"they want me to disappear, like it's gonna shift for them."
Already Home
The Blueprint 3

when you're doing well and your spot is reserved, you'll start to see more people start to come for your head in an attempt to get attention and secure a spot for themselves. these people have convinced themselves that you are the only thing standing between them and where they want to be. it might be relationships. you might have the boyfriend or girlfriend they wish they had. it might be professional. you might have the job that they want. hell, it may even be something petty like you have the wardrobe they want. or are you the person that has fixated on someone else and decided that they are getting in your way? no one else can stop what god has determined is for you. stop the sucker shit. regardless of which side of the fence you're on, keep doing you. keep putting in the effort and you'll see the outcome reflected in what you put in. claim it.

i am secure.

september 8
"take a leap of faith and let my eagle wings spread."
So Ambitious
The Blueprint 3

what do you daydream about? are you working towards it? or are you just hoping for the things you dream about to mysteriously appear? if you're not working to make it happen, why not? what the hell are you waiting for? what are you afraid of? if you allow your fears to supersede your faith, you've already failed. don't clip your wings before you have a chance to fly. there is nowhere to go but up. fly.

i have faith in my abilities.

september 9
“what your future do? and we don't really care what you used to say, unless that affects your future pay.”
Off That
The Blueprint 3

are you living in the past? i know you’ve heard that saying “what have you done for me, lately?” well, what have you done? for others? for yourself? stop reminiscing about things that aren’t pushing you to your potential, but instead, preventing you from it. be propelled by your past. of course, it’s fun to talk about the good ole days, but make sure your best days are ahead of you, not behind you. do things today that your future self will thank you for.

i am focused on my future.

september 10
“divine intervention, y'all can't prevent me from shining.”
Nigga Please
The Blueprint 2: The Gift & The Curse

don’t allow people to get in the way of your goals. no matter who it is or what they say, just do it. you owe it to yourself. don’t concern yourself with what others are doing or not doing, saying or not saying, just focus on doing what you have to do. your belief in yourself and your own abilities is what is most important. if you think you can, you will. you will find a way. if you think you can’t, then you won’t. you will find an excuse. don’t let others stand in the way of your goals. push pass the objections and make your way out of the shadows and into the sunshine.

what is meant for me will be for me.

september 11
"unless you was me, how could you judge me?"
Blueprint²
The Blueprint 2: The Gift & The Curse

are you free from sin? probably not. you may have attempted to rationalize the gravity of those sins or explain what drove you to make those decisions. so, what gives you permission to judge others for their sins? i'm sure most people can justify the bad things they've done with the bad things that have happened to them. who determines what's right and what's wrong? who decides who's the victim and who's the victimizer? not everyone shares their battles with the outside world. try being more sympathetic to others, especially if you'd want someone to show you compassion during trying times.

only god can judge me.

september 11
"fortune 5, top 5 in the forbes, you'll see. as y'all thumb through the source, i read the robb report."
Only A Customer
Streets is Watching

what's on your vision board? what do you intend to make of your life? what things are you doing to fuel your passions and realize your vision. what are you reading? who are you networking with? what projects are you working on? who are you surrounding yourself with? are you doing your research? if you stay ready, you ain't gotta get ready. keep your thoughts positive and stay informed and aware in order to stay inspired and ensure that your dreams become plans and those plans turn into action that transforms your reality.

i create the life i want.

september 12
“i guess it's just the penalty of leadership. i guess i'm what niggaz want to be and shit, or niggaz just bored, want to be in shit.”
Some People Hate
The Blueprint 2: The Gift & The Curse

when you’re at the front people will try to pull you back for various reasons. Sometimes, they want your spot, other times they just don’t want you to have and other times they just want to be associated with someone who is on top even if it’s on the opposing side. being on top and doing well demands that you are strong because you can guarantee that people will test you. how will you respond? Will you give them the attention that they’re looking for or will you keep your attention fixed firmly in the direction of your goals?

i realize that some people will detest my success. i will succeed anyway.

september 13
“i'm representing for the seat where rosa parks sat where malcolm x was shot, where martin luther was popped.”
The Ruler's Back
The Blueprint

how well do you know your history? not just what you were taught in school, but have you done your own research? do you watch documentaries, read books and go to museums? do you talk to your grandparents? understanding history can offer perspective about the present and insight into the future. it allows you understanding of how you got to where you are and who and what was sacrificed for you to have the things that you have today. nothing is given to you in this world. if you want it, you have got to take it and you have got to do the work to hold on to it or you’ll find that it has slipped through your fingers.

i am my ancestors wildest dreams.

september 14
"being broke is a great motivator."
Jonathan Ross Show
6/27/2008

have you ever been poor? have you ever hit hard times? it happens. there may be times when you have more than enough, and life is good and there may be other times when you don't know where your next dollar is coming from. being afflicted with these conditions can sometimes be a part of life. tough time don't last. however, these times should make you tougher. you have two options: either get comfortable being broke or allow the discomfort to fuel your hustle. when you don't have, i'm sure you've gotten creative on ways to ear and hold on to the little that you have. don't give in to tough times, demonstrate that you are tougher.

i am driven by my environment.

september 15
“don't only talk it, walk like it.”
The Ruler's Back
The Blueprint

do you know someone that’s always talking about what they’re going to do? its irritating, isn’t it? you know why? because somehow, they never seem to do the things that they spent so much time talking about. or, if they actually do it, you realize that the stories about it were so much better than the execution. don’t be this person. don’t over promise and underdeliver. work you plan and shock the world with your strides. be known for doing it big, not for dreaming big. make sure your words are aligned with your actions.

i let my actions speak for me.

september 16
"it's like bringing a knife to a gunfight, pen to a test."
Takeover
The Blueprint

did you ever show up to school in your best outfit only to remember that you have a paper due? have you ever gone on a job interview without researching the company? i'm sure you felt like a real screw up. i bet you made sure never made that mistake again, didn't you? success happens when preparation meets opportunity. always know what you're up against and prepare accordingly. being prepared allows for confidence that will contribute to you doing your absolute best. do your homework, sharpen your pencils, stretch. do the things necessary to set you up for success.

i am prepared.

september 17
"a wise man told me don't argue with fools. cause people from a distance can't tell who is who."
Takeover
The Blueprint

how frustrating is it to have a disagreement with an ignorant person? Ignorant, by definition, means to be uninformed or unaware. what's worse is that they don't even realize how foolish they are, and they relentlessly argue their point with the passion of someone who knows what they're talking about. when you fight with facts, its unnecessary to engage with ignorant people. they will only bring you down to their level. don't come off your thrown to address peasants. if they believe 1 plus 1 equals three, they are correct. next.

i stop talking when i've proved my point.

september 18
"faced with immeasurable odds, still I gave straight bets."
Where I'm From
In My Lifetime ... Vol 1

life is a gamble. unfortunately, we can't control the hand that we've been dealt, but it is up to us to play the hell out of that hand every single time. sometimes it may feel like there is no way out, but you've got to persevere and think smart and figure out the work-around. the greater the obstacle, the greater the glory. may the odds forever be in your favor.

i bet on myself.

september 19
"the purest form of giving is anonymous to anonymous."
Nickels And Dimes
Magna Carta ... Holy Grail

have you ever had someone help you and you were super grateful until you learned that they've boasted about what they've done for you? it almost makes you want to go back in time and decline their help. have you ever been the one that bragged about helping someone in need? do you volunteer and take pictures of the needy? do you give the man on the corner a dollar and make him take a picture for it? imagine the impossible position that this person has been put in. do they turn down the much-needed assistance or pose for the camera? think about why you have decided to help someone. is it for bragging rights or do you really want to make a difference?

i allow my good deeds to speak for me.

september 20
"you could've been anywhere in the world, but you're here with me, i appreciate that."
Izzo
The Blueprint

do you have a friend that spends all your time together on their phone? they might be on social media scrolling through their newsfeed, checking work emails complaining about passive aggressive co-workers, or texting other friends. it's so frustrating! it's like when you go to a restaurant to place your order but the person that calls over the phone takes priority over you. you're giving them your undivided attention and they seemingly have better things to do. the disrespect is real. you don't know how much time you have, so every moment spent is precious. if you knew you only had a day to live, how much of that time would you spend with people that are scrolling on their timeline?

i respect others time.

september 21
"can't knock the hustle."
Can't Knock The Hustle
Reasonable Doubt

you ever notice how so many people seem to look strippers in judgment but think it's cool to be a pimp? they will celebrate gangsters and look down on janitors. what's that about? if something hasn't been romanticized in the movies it has been determined as an unacceptable means of feeding your family. the cost of living is real, and it is steadily increasing. somehow, it costs to do everything. some companies have even found ways to charge for oxygen. survival is costly and you are responsible for those bills that you accumulate. no one else. don't allow anyone to shame you for what you have to do to keep the rent paid, the lights on and food on the table. someone who wants to judge will find a way to do so whether you're working 3 jobs or swinging on a pole. before knocking someone's hustle, consider if you're willing to help them pay their bills before you start in on them. then put your money where your mouth is.

i respect how others fulfill their needs.

september 22
“pay us like you owe us for all the years that you hoed us.”
Izzo
The Blueprint

have you ever noticed the equal opportunity employer disclaimer on job applications? why do you think that’s there? is it mandated? does it give you confidence in the company that you’re applying to or working for? do you think their hiring practices are honest and fair? how about how they distribute compensation packages? you get what you negotiate. so, with so many examples of unfair and unequal treatment and compensation, what will you do to make sure you enter negotiations armed with the tools to get what you want and do a solid to the people that have been taken advantage of?

i get what i negotiate.

september 23
"we can talk, but money talks, so talk mo' bucks."
Izzo
The Blueprint

how are your negotiation skills? i'm sure you've heard, you get what you negotiate. it's true. no matter what you're worth, if you terrible at negotiations you can easily be taken advantage of. you need to know what you deserve and set out to get it. do your research. think big picture. how much do you have the potential to earn? make a play and make it happen. don't allow people to continuously waste your time setting meetings that never lead to projects or with budgets that don't justify your involvement. find a way to make things work for you or find someone else to do business with.

it's business, never personal.

september 24
"Hov is back, life stories told through rap."
Izzo
The Blueprint

the game is to be sold, not to be told. vultures can only rob the culture if you keep giving it away. in some cases, our culture is all we have to bring to the table. so, are you going to recognize how valuable your life experiences are and protect your treasure or continue giving away your stories and buying them back from the very people you gave them to for free? you've got to use what you've got to get what you want? think hard. what do you have? what do you want? how can you leverage what you know, who you know and what you're good at to get from point a to point b?

i know my value.

september 25
“to try and to fail: the two things i hate.”
Izzo
The Blueprint

the surest way to fail at something is to not even try. interestingly, lots of people seem to think that that’s the way to avoid failure. not true. if you haven’t tried, you’ve already failed. if you try, you’re guaranteed to get a result that is beneficial to you, even if it’s not the result you were hoping for. at the very least, you learn a valuable lesson that can help you navigate your future attempts. when you’ve never done something before you generally go into it blind which increases the probability that you might make some mistakes. when you’re mining for gold, you might step on some land mines. risk the possibility of failing big for the possibility of achieving bigger. learn valuable lessons and become better with each attempt.

i either win or learn.

september 26
“she like, "listen Jigga man, i don't care if you rap, you better r-e-s-p-e-c-t me."
Girls, Girls, Girls
The Blueprint

there are people that develop an inflated sense of self-importance based on their accomplishments. so much so that they begin to treat others in a demeaning way. they can be dismissive or verbally abusive. you have to decide that you will not tolerate disrespect. from anyone. it is simply unacceptable. just because someone may be important, it doesn’t make you unimportant. treat people how you want to be treated and be clear on how you expect to be treated. there are no exceptions. once you let someone slide, they start skating. either they respect it, or you check it.

i demand respect.

september 27
"ride with me, get high as me. it's how it's supposed to be, when you rolling with g's, Hov'!"
Jigga That Nigga
The Blueprint

do you have a friend that is doing well? have you ever tried to do business with them? or are they content with keeping their personal relationships separate from their professional relationships? are there synergies in what you do? have there been opportunities to work together or make money together, yet they refuse? first, check yourself. have you shown some traits that make you look like a terrible colleague? if not, and you've been on your grind and excelling in your industry, pitch your project to your potential partner. dot all of your i's and cross your t's. if they're as official as you think, they won't ignore a great opportunity to make an impact together.

i am my brother's keeper.

september 28
"bite your tongue for no one and whatever is said is said, take it how they want. a closed mouth don't get fed."
Anything
The Truth (Beanie Siegel)

it's been said that the truth will set you free, but trust and believe that most people can't handle the truth. regardless, speak your truth. say what it is and be clear about who you are and what you want. it's unfair of others to expect you to hold your tongue or project alternative facts to comfort them. if people don't like it when you keep it real, those aren't your people. as long as your intentions aren't malicious, the truth wins. find people that value transparency and understand that the truth and authenticity are powerful. it doesn't change. it is what it is, no matter what they want it to be. keep honest people around you that are not afraid to tell you what they think. this will allow you to stay true to yourself and stay on track with who said you are, what you said you want to be and what you want from life.

it is what it is and i am who i am.

september 29
"he did it again! haters no like but they gotta fuck with it cause the flow is so tight."
Jigga That Nigga
The Blueprint

be so good that your haters can't ignore you. give them something to talk about. they're going to talk anyway, so you might as well control the conversation. when you're good you can't be denied. i'm sure that there are songs by artists that you don't like that you can't help but sing along to. it's the same thing in whatever it is you're trying to do. when you're great, you're great. no one can take your greatness away from you. it's who you are at your core. its undeniable. they'll eventually come around. your worst critic can one day easily become your biggest fan. filter through the criticisms and find the ones that are constructive and allow them to help you improve and perfect your craft. keep pushing, keep believing. keep improving. be great.

i won't be denied.

september 30
"put me anywhere on god's green earth, i'll triple my worth."
You Don't Know
The Blueprint

if you come here with nothing, it is not your fault, but if you leave with nothing, you are to blame. ask yourself what you did with the time you were allotted. your time here should be spent putting numbers on the board. shoot your shot. follow your passions. use your skills. there is nowhere to go but up. it's up to you to keep climbing. what are you good at? what have you experienced? what have you learned? what have you built? where have you been? what will you do? who have you influenced? what are you working on? what are you planning? everything you do should be adding to, not subtracting from. pour into the world, pour into people. make history by making some things happen. get to it!

i invest in myself.

october 1
"one life to live, notice you get no sequel. so i truly got to live this like my last movie."
Hola Hovito
The Blueprint

as far as we know, this is the only life that we're going to get. we don't know how long this life will be, nor do we know how it will end. it varies for different people. some of us will live shorter lives than others and have an impact so great that our names will ring for centuries to come. Tupac died at 25 years old. Biggie didn't make it to his 25th birthday. MLK was 39 and Malcolm X didn't make it to his 40th birthday. it's not when you die, but what you do while you're alive. wake up and make history. do things that will impact the minds and lives of others. put your all into whatever you do. seize the days and the opportunities. it's your life and its only one per person. make it count.

i live a life worth living.

october 2
"our time together is our time together and our time apart is our time apart."
Girls, Girls, Girls (Part 2)
The Blueprint

in life you'll meet lots of people. you'll know some longer than others. you'll meet some early in life, some later. some will leave, some will stay, and some will just be temporary encounters. each of these people will leave an impression on you, no matter how small. you might notice someone's style. you might be touched by someone's smile. or you might be nurtured by someone's love and secured by someone's dependability. these people will help develop you. so, why do we sometimes become possessive about our loved ones to the point that we smother them? we act as if there are the limits to how many people you can love and rules about how much time you are required to spend with them. you don't own people, you experience them. instead of living in the moment and enjoying the time we have with our loved ones, we concern ourselves with who else they're giving their time to, instead of dedicating your time without them to people and things that are also important to you.

i value my time with others.

october 3
“even though y'all hate i love y'all muhfuckers friend or foe, y'all all my muhfuckers.”
Hola Hovito
The Blueprint

there will always be people that don’t like you, hell, even people that hate you. it’s been said that hate is confused admiration. all they know is you make them feel a way and they don’t like that feeling. your dopeness might be making them feel less than. who you are might make them realize everything they’re not and possibly some things they want to be. you can’t control how you make them feel simply by being you. and if you’re as dope as they secretly think you are i’m sure their hatred, in part, is because of how other people show you love. remember, you can only hate someone as much as you love them, and only love kills hate. so, choose love.

i love my haters.

october 4
“i'm a hustler homey, you a customer crony.”
Dirt Off Your Shoulder
The Black Album

look up and down. what are you wearing? who are you wearing? look around you? where did all the things surrounding you come from? what are you creating and producing? or are you just being sold to by everyone else. wouldn’t you rather have an additional stream of income coming in than to have your limited income always going out because you’re purchasing things that are aligned with trends that you help set? stop playing it safe.

i provide the wave.

october 5
"they say they never really miss you 'til you dead or you gone."
December 4th
The Black Album

when someone passes away, everyone is sorry for the loss and wishes that they rest in peace. the funny thing is that most of those people probably clashed with the deceased when they were alive. probably went weeks, months or even years without talking to them or maybe talking bad about them. how often do your friends and family say good things about you to you? when was the last time you showed someone you love them? are you a supportive friend? how often do you send flowers? somehow, after someone has died people's regret for their shady behavior makes it a lot easier to express their feelings of gratitude and see past the bullshit. are you guilty of the same behavior? if you love someone, get over yourself and treat every day like it's your last or as if it might be theirs. don't get so caught up in the stuff that doesn't really matter.

i'm grateful for the people in my life.

october 6
"but every time i hit the ground i bounce up like round ball."
Heart Of The City
The Blueprint

things happen. things will challenge you. things will challenge your faith. things will challenge your strength. things will challenge your character. things will challenge your beliefs. it's how your respond to those challenges that show you what you're really made of. will you break? will you snap? will you lose sight of what's important? or will you keep your eyes on the prize and mindfully choose to not be distracted or discouraged by life's challenges? will you choose to accept the challenge and take it as an opportunity to grow stronger in the areas you may be weak in? will you shift your perspective and elect to see the opportunity presented in each circumstance? whatever happens, keep going. keep believing. no matter how many times you fall, get back up.

i refuse to stay down.

october 7
“we all fish, better teach ya folk. give em money to eat, then next week he's broke. cause when you sleep, he's reaching for your throat.”
Never Change
The Blueprint

who are you surrounded by? what do they bring to the table? what are you bringing to the table? does each of you offer something that you can teach the other to make each other better? to help each other grow? to allow each other to be self-sufficient and to make your group stronger as a whole? do you have multiple streams of income? do you have a guaranteed way to feed yourself? do you know how to farm or fish? do you own land? will you always have a roof over your head? how about your friends and family? if you’re all not equipped with the proper skills and tools, someone may be forced to rely on the other. if your only way of getting things when you’re depleted is by asking someone else for help, you’ll always be dependent. dependency can be to your detriment. pay attention and take note and make sure your people know how to swim, so they won’t sink.

i am my brother’s teacher.

october 8
“chains is cool a cop but more important is lawyer fees.”
Never Change
The Blueprint

what’s your plan? are you saving for retirement? do you plan to work until you die? are you prepared for an emergency? or do you spend your money before it’s made and save nothing? there is absolutely nothing wrong with indulging your wants, but overindulging is an entirely different story. are you regularly putting aside a piece of the pie in a rainy-day fund? if you overspend on your wants and neglect your savings and investments, you’ll be left scrambling in your time of need.

i am prepared.

october 9
“old heads taught me youngin' walk softly.”
Never Change
The Blueprint

how have you learned all the things you know now? i’m sure a good deal of the things you know were taught to you by other people. people older and wiser than us pass on the lessons they’ve learned from people older and wiser than them and from their own experiences. having a coach makes it easier to make a play the game. They see things you don’t. learn from others than can see the big picture and potential threats to your wellbeing and the achievement of your goals.

i learn from my elders’ experiences.

october 10
"the streets robbed me wasn't educated properly."
Never Change
The Blueprint

the misinformation we pick up from unreliable sources can misguide our steps. this is also true for the lack of information. so many people stop reading and stop seeking information once school ends and are content with remaining ignorant. it's almost like they don't see the value in being informed. i guess ignorance really is bliss. the truth hurts, so if you don't know the difficult truth it's easy to feel overwhelmed. it has also been said that the truth will set you free. free from what? possibly the limits of your mind. don't impose an expiration date on your education. the mind is a terrible thing to waste.

i understand that ignorance is not bliss.

october 11
"knocked a nigga of his feet but i crawled back."
Never Change
The Blueprint

in life, you'll have to fight for the things you want. keep swinging. sometimes you might take a hit. keep swinging. sometimes you may get knocked down. get up and keep swinging. for as long as you have a life to live, you've got to give it the good fight. no matter how tough things may seem, know that you are tougher. you are made stronger by each thing that you have gone toe to toe with. you've proven that the trials are no match for you.

i won't give up.

october 12
"get your swag back, daddy. where your focus at?"
Kingdom Come
Kingdom Come

every now and then, life might get to you. there are peaks and valleys. sometimes you're up, other times you're down. there is nothing to be ashamed of. you might miss your beat occasionally, but don't ever lose your rhythm. Queue up your theme music and get your head out of the clouds. stop playing around and get back to work. are you spending too much time partying and bullshitting? stop living your best life and get back to being your best self. work on yourself. work on your projects. start slaying your goals and stop wasting your time. there are lots of things you said you'd do and the person you said you'd become is waiting. don't fall off, put yourself on.

i am focused.

october 13
"death before dishonor, correct? yep."
Never Change
The Blueprint

loyalty can have different definitions depending upon who you talk to. people have their own definition of loyalty. that's why it's so hard to find it in others these days. you need to understand a person's morals and values to have some insight as to their code of conduct. what do you talk about? what do your conversations with them tell you about them? how do they behave? are they solid? do their actions match their words? do their words match their thoughts? how can someone be disloyal or dishonor your relationship if you never understood the code? it's easy to break a rule or agreement that you don't know exists. get to know people and what they're about before calling them your friends. understand who they are, not just who they say they are to be clear that they stick to the script.

i honor myself and others.

october 14
"only Christopher we acknowledge is Wallace."
Oceans
Magna Carta ... Holy Grail

who do you celebrate? what do you celebrate? what makes those things worthy of your celebration? are you just going with the flow and following the crowd or are you informed? what makes something or someone worthy of your attention and support? do you look at their character? do you consider their accomplishments? do you examine their faults? does their action or inaction have to directly benefit you? take some time think about the people and things you celebrate and ask yourself why you've chosen to celebrate them. then think about the people you admire. the events in history that you deem monumental. you may decide that you'll start celebrating Juneteenth with a day off and a feast.

i choose my own heroes.

october 15
"you will get return in your investment if attention you pay."
Guns & Roses
The Blueprint 2: The Gift & The Curse

what you get out of things is a direct result of what you put into them. are you putting your all in it or are you doing things half-ass? are you practicing? are you working hard? are you learning? are you focused? are you disciplined? you can't expect monumental results from minimal effort. there is a difference between working smart and being lazy. keep your mind on your business. take note of what you spend your time doing and what you give your attention to. what are you getting out of it?

i am paying attention.

october 16
"but when it turns your way before it turns away gotta turn that into something you gotta learn from Jay."
Guns & Roses
The Blueprint 2: The Gift & The Curse

seize the day. luck is when preparedness meets opportunity. if you stay ready, you don't have to get ready when the thing that you have been preparing for comes to fruition. for instance, if you've been hoping for summer, are you spending each day getting summer ready? are you in the gym? are you eating right? are you putting together your summer wardrobe? are you planning vacations? have you saved your coins? it's like jumping double dutch, be ready to jump in when you have an opening.

i take advantage of the opportunities that i'm presented.

october 17
"mo' money, mo' problems" gotta move carefully."
Heart Of The City
The Blueprint

it's easy to think that money can solve all your problems when you don't have any. the day-to-day stress that most people face can be connected to the bills that they've accumulated to live the life they want. the truth is, you don't really want more money, you just want to live the life you want to live. even with money, there are some problems you can't solve. you might have a roof over your head and food in your stomach, but your husband and children may still be stressing you out. or your health may be poor. then there's the possibility that you may now have problems associated with having money, like not being able to responsibly manage it, protecting yourself from thieves, and knowing who you can trust. money isn't the answer to all things. you can't throw sugar on shit and expect i to digest well. be careful what you ask for and be sure you are prepared to handle it.

money does not solve all of my problems, i do.

october 18
"i run the streets, the streets don't we."
Kingdom Come
Kingdom Come

somewhere along the lines the rules got blurred and the code was broken. do you speak to others as you walk past them? do you look out for others safety and wellbeing? do you support others? respect them? do you keep your community safe? do you put people on? do you give back? chances are, these things are all things that you expect of and hope for in others. so, what's the problem? you can't complain about times changing and the world being crazy if you're a part of the craziness. there was a time when we knew our neighbors and looked out for them. that's what created community. we poured into each other because we understood that we are all we've got. you must embody the things you want to be reflected in society and be the solution instead of being a part of the problem. stop complaining about what is wrong with the world and how people don't respect the rules. instead, wake up every day rule the world. consciously decide to act with intention and be the change you want to see. the world is yours to develop.

i make the rules.

october 19
"young'uns ice-grilling me. oh, you not feeling me? fine, it cost you nothing, pay me no mind."
Heart Of The City
The Blueprint

why do people put so much energy into people and things that they don't like? if you don't like someone, you'll tell anyone who will listen about them. why? is this an attempt to convince others that that person should not be liked or trusted? if you like someone, you generally keep it to yourself. why? are you trying to keep that person to yourself? if you don't like your food, do you keep eating it and complaining about it or do you push it aside and find something that you do like? practice the same behavior with people. stop giving your attention to things you don't like. stop complaining about the people that don't show up to your party. its disrespectful to the people you like and the people that like you. the world could do without all the negativity and bad energy. move on and get over it.

i pay attention to things that make me feel good.

october 20
“sensitive thugs, y'all all need hugs.”
Heart Of The City
The Blueprint

we all know someone that can dish it out but can’t take it. we’re constantly baffled at how a person can talk so aggressively to others or behave so insensitively but expect that other people to talk and act nice to them. what’s up with that? people’s actions are a huge indicator as to what’s going on inside them and what they’ve been through in their lives. hurt people, hurt people. aggression is often perceived to be associated with strength and masculinity, but no one generally takes the time to understand the root of that behavior. not even the person displaying it. in so many communities, therapy is decidedly for the weak instead a necessary tool for healing your weaknesses. are you working on healing your hurt to ensure that you don’t hurt others?

i am healing.

october 21
"as fate would have it, JAY'z status appears to be at an all-time high, perfect time to say goodbye. when i come back like jordan it ain't to play games with you."
Encore
The Black Album

all things must come to an end. that's just the way things work. the sun sets. milk spoils. buildings crumble. All men die. how many relationships have you had? things fall apart. how many places have you been? you have to get back to life. how many jobs have you had? move onward and upward. you have to leave things and people better than you found them. do you know how to go out on top and pass the baton when your time is up? do you want to be remembered for all the good you've done and allow others the opportunity to long for your return or will you be the last one to leave the party? solidify yourself as an unforgettable character in the minds and hearts of others and don't wear out your welcome. people will long for your presence and when you wish to return, you will be welcomed back with open arms.

i will go out on top.

october 22
"what you eat don't make me shit."
Heart Of The City
The Blueprint

if you keep your eyes on someone else's plate, your own food will get cold. how much time do you spend talking about what someone else is doing, good or bad, instead working on your own plan? do you have a plan? are you working it? use others as inspiration or as cautionary tales of what not do. don't waste away your precious time with gossip. generally, what other people are doing with their lives doesn't directly affect the people that are consumed with talking about them. so, why do you think they commit so much time with keeping up with jones? boredom? jealously? either way, those problems can be solved easily by working on your own shit. decide to mind your own business and you won't have much time to be consumed by other people's business. just enough time to congratulate them on their wins and encourage them during their lessons.

i am not distracted by things that have nothing to do with me.

october 23
"and a drought can define a man, when the well dries up."
December 4th
The Black Album

how you act when you have nothing and when you have everything are true character defining moments. when your back is against the wall, what will you do? will you come out swinging? will you make a way out of no way? will you sink or swim? think about a tough time when you thought you wouldn't survive. what did you do to save yourself? a lot of us know that there is no other option to make things happen with the pressure is on. when pressure is applied, it can either cause an individual to fold or create a diamond. what doesn't kill you will strengthen you as long as you don't stop fighting. don't get overwhelmed by the tides, learn to swim.

i can swim.

october 24
“and it's nobody fault, i made the decisions i made. this is the life i chose, or rather the life that chose me.”
December 4th
The Black Album

you and only you are responsible for the choices you make that affect your life. now, it may be true that at some point you did not choose the situations that presented you with one bad option after another. but it is up to you to make the decision because you have to live with the results. making a decision that ultimately positively impacts the greater good, may negatively affect you and vice versa. you have to live with the results and the regrets. separate the pros from the cons and make a decision and deal with the repercussions.

i take accountability for my life.

october 25
"time waits for no man. can't turn back the hands once it's too late."
Regrets
Reasonable Doubt

what are you waiting for? tomorrow? next week? next year? what makes you so sure that you'll be around then? if you are, what makes you sure that you'll have the capabilities to do the things that you're putting off? you aren't certain. none of us are. none of us can be. take advantage of opportunities while you can. take that trip. apply to that job. call that girl. learn that skill. tell someone you miss them. stop assuming that you have time. once the moment is gone, you can't get it back. don't continue wasting the time that you do have. it may very well be your last day. if that were true, what would you do? hypothetically, assume for a moment that you only have 24 hours to live. how much time would you spend sleeping? how much tv would you watch? probably, very little. go out and live your life! make a to-do list and get busy checking things off the list. the time is now.

i am seizing the moment.

october 26
"so, picture me letting these clowns nitpick at me. paint me like a pickney."
What More Can I Say
The Black Album

do you care what others think of you? why? who are they? who assigned them as judge and jury? why do you honor their opinion? man, fuck these people. why does their opinion of you matter more to you than what you know about you? this is your life. you can't shake yourself. you are with you 24 hours a day, 7 days a week, 365 days a year... 366 in a leap year. you, and only you know your heart. only you know your thoughts. you are not responsible for how others interpret you. you are only responsible for what you represent. for what energy you put out into the world. for the value that you add to others. don't be distracted by the noise. be confident in your knowledge of self.

i am not defined by what others think of me.

october 27

"they giveth and they taketh life is cruel that way but even a broken clock is right at least two times a day."
Guns & Roses
The Blueprint 2: The Gift & The Curse

nothing is permanent. sometimes you will have, sometimes you will have not. don't get too cocky and think that what you have gained cannot be lost. be grateful. show grace. appreciate your blessings. you will not always have the answer. there are times you will be right and times you will be wrong. be humble. keep an open mind. learn from others. when you're down, work on earning and learning and when you're up share what you've acquired.

i will have my time to shine.

october 28
"i got my shades on waiting for the sun to shine my way."
Guns & Roses
The Blueprint 2: The Gift & The Curse

do you believe in luck? Or are you prepared for opportunities. are you expecting the things you want to happen? do you educate yourself and seek out opportunities in preparation for the job of your dreams? are you working on being your best self in anticipation of one day finding a mate. if you think money grows on trees, are you planting and watering seeds? or are you just waiting for something to happen to you with no effort on your part? if you fail to prepare, you better be prepared to fail. one day, your chance will come. will you be prepared?

i am prepared for all lucrative opportunities.

october 29
"they say when you play with skills, good luck could happen."
Guns & Roses
The Blueprint 2: The Gift & The Curse

what are you good at? what do you like to do? do you work on improving those skills or do you take them for granted? the things that you're good at are your gift from the universe that you should be sharing with the world. it's what makes you special. that's why it comes so easily to you. but you must practice it. practicing is your acknowledgment of your ability. if you take it for granted, you'll risk losing your ability and the opportunities that may be brought about by those skills. practice basketball every day. go to dance class. work on your mathematics. if you like playing video games, learn to create them. work on your art. take voice lessons or cooking classes. whatever it is you're good at, do it. do it well and watch your life get better.

my skills take me where i'm trying to go.

october 30
"i'm learning all the potholes in every single barrio. trying not to mess up my axis kid."
Guns & Roses
The Blueprint 2: The Gift & The Curse

throughout life's ups and downs, you are constantly being presented with teachable moments. those times where you trip, and maybe even fall, are really opportunities to see where you may have gone wrong and avoid similar situations in the future. they are also reminders to pay attention. i'm sure there are potholes is your city. you probably know the ones you pass everyday like the back of your hand. you know when to proceed with caution and when to change lanes. these things can cost you time and money and make you a more defensive driver. unless you forget the impact and recklessly plow ahead. life is a lot like this. watch your step and pay attention along your journey so you don't get unnecessarily derailed.

i learn from my mistakes.

october 31
"flowers need water to grow, it gotta rain and in order to experience joy you need pain."
Guns & Roses
The Blueprint 2: The Gift & The Curse

rain can slow down your plans, but it can also water your plants. it's all about your perspective. instead of singing rain, rain go away so you can go outside and play, use the time to check some things off your to-do list to move closer to your goals. sometimes, when it rains it pours. things may happen in your life that really knock the wind out of you. you may lose a job, go through a breakup or lose a friend or family member. instead of focusing on the pain, try to find the good. push through the pain. what did those things teach you? how did you grow? allow these tough moments to make you better, so you can see better day.

i'm watered by rain.

november 1
"i swear; i only make good from my mouth to god's ears."
Diamond Is Forever
The Blueprint 2: The Gift & The Curse

when you put it in god's hands do you also do your part? or do you just send prayers up and sit back and wait for all of the things you asked for? faith without work is dead. if you're not making good on the things you're asking god for, then not only are you breaking your agreement with god, but you're also breaking the agreement with yourself about what you want from life. you've got to do your part. do what you can do and let god handle the rest. you can't expect the cake to be baked if you never mixed the ingredients. after you've done all you can, do a little more and allow the most high to work magic. have faith and work your plan.

i do the work.

november 2
"nobody gave us shit, we made us."
I Did It My Way
The Blueprint 2: The Gift & The Curse

sometimes you have to create a way out of no way. nobody owes you anything. use what you have to get what you want. dig deep. what resources are available to you? who's on your team? what are they good at? what resources do they have? put your heads together and come up with a plan to make something happen. leave no stone unturned. don't sit around waiting for a handout. no one is coming to save you. it is up to you to save yourself. it is up to you to do the work to make your dreams become reality. no one will ever give you what you're worth. they will only give you enough to quiet your dreams and use your skills to fulfill someone else's. when you go after the things you want, the risks are big and so are the rewards. how sweet it is to be able to say you created something that will forever change your life and the lives of those involved. make it happen.

i will do it my way.

november 3
“you know what they say about he who hesitates in war, he who hesitates is lost.”
Meet The Parents
The Blueprint 2: The Gift & The Curse

how many times have you said, “i’ll do it tomorrow” or “i’ll do it next week”? what are you waiting for? stop procrastinating. why put off tile tomorrow what you can do today? if you are not willing to leave this earth without having done it, do it now. take the chance. do your best. get it done. cross it off your list. see what comes of it. if you don’t take advantage of the opportunities that are presented to you, someone else will. don’t let what’s meant for you, lap you. get ready now and be prepared so you don’t fumble when the opportunity comes around. how would you feel watching someone else step up and live your dream because you took the opportunity for granted and didn’t snatch it up when it was in front of you? don’t be a slave to your fears or your procrastination. just do it.

i move with intention.

november 4
"i'm from the streets where the hood could swallow a man, bullets will follow a man."
U Don't Know
The Blueprint 2: The Gift & The Curse

how complicated was your childhood? did you have it rough? was your neighborhood rough? it looks like you survived, and guess what? only the strong survive. along the way, you surely picked up some survival tactics. can you sense danger? can you read people and situations? these skills are transferable. not only did they help navigate your neighborhood, but they should also help you navigate the world, which is undoubtedly much crazier and on a larger scale. instead of allowing your environment to bury you, let it cultivate you and push you to your greatness.

i am tough.

november 5
"politics as usual"
Politics As Usual
Reasonable Doubt

politics requires the participation of all that are affected by the decisions. it is a what's in it for me industry. unfortunately, most of those asking what's in for me are those that are supposed to be representing the people. the agreement is that if i do x, you'll do y. however, too many people are giving away their vote without any expectations, agreements or holding others accountable for fulfilling their part of the agreement. can you imagine paying someone your money and never receiving anything in return? sounds crazy, right? politics has the potential to change your reality, but you first must be sure you have people in place that are working in the best interest of the community. otherwise, they end up working against you. make sure the people you put to work are doing their job and those that you are giving power are using that power appropriately.

my actions are reciprocated.

november 6
"for playing me y'all shall forever remain nameless."
U Don't Know
The Blueprint 2: The Gift & The Curse

when you make it to the top there will be lots of people coming out of the woodwork trying to get your attention. they will be trying to ride your wave and make a name for themselves. they may be trying to work with you or work against you. either way, they're looking to benefit from your success. these may be people you couldn't get ahold when you were grinding, they may be people you'd met along the way, and others you may not even know or know of. suddenly, people that didn't believe you initially are now believers and in other cases you may have some so-called enemies that are hoping to get you to respond and validate them. it is up to you whether those people succeed with their motives. why not keep the same energy? you made it this far without their involvement. why allow them to make a name for themselves off of your name that you worked so hard to establish. allow your indifference to these people to guide your response and use your silence in the same way that you would use your words.

i uplift my believers, not my naysayers.

november 7
"seen the worst of the worst i deserve every blessing i received i'm from the dirt."
Some How Some Way
The Blueprint 2: The Gift & The Curse

when you come from nothing, you are grateful for every blessing you receive. having nothing humbles you. since you know what it's like to have so little or not have at all, you are appreciative of every change in your circumstances. each day that you wake up is a blessing. you've seen so many others not make it to see a new day that you don't take each day for granted. You take advantage of each opportunity presented to you because you understand that it is a chance to improve your predicament. you understand that blessings are not always monetary. sometimes it may be having food in your pantry, having heat on a cold day or having clean water to drink. don't take life's blessings for granted. someone else is praying for the things that you disregard. each day be thankful for what you have been given, be motivated by your lack of and give the world all you have and the most high will bless you with what you deserve.

i understand each day is a blessing.

november 8
"i planted my seed on unfertile land myrtle, park. marcy, flushing and nostrand and still i grew somehow i knew the sun will shine through."
Somehow Some Way
The Blueprint 2: The Gift & The Curse

life is like a card game and it is up to you to play the hand that you've been dealt. since you can't control the hand that you've been dealt, don't spend your time complaining about the hand you've got. make something out of nothing. it's not the hand you've got, but the person holding the cards. so, bet on yourself. you know what outcome to be, right? you want to win. so, win! play your hand. play it with such precision, that it'll appear as if you've got the exact hand you hoped for. practice your poker face, until it just becomes your face. use what you've be given to get the outcome you want.

i will tend to my garden.

november 9

"he was just some thug that, caught some slugs and we loved him cause, in him we, saw some of us. he walked like us, talked like us his back against the wall, nigga fought like us."
Meet The Parents
The Blueprint 2: The Gift & The Curse

representation matters. the election and presidency of Barrack Obama allowed a lot of little black kids the opportunity to dream that they too might one day be president of the united states or first lady. something that had before never been realistically considered by people of color. as records continue to be broken and firsts continue to be accomplished, each accomplishment offers a glimmer of hope to the underdogs that they are capable. seeing your image in people in successful and powerful positions is like looking in the mirror. people can generally only see their options in what they see. So, if you only see "success" in one-of-a-kind athletes and those that have elected to take a criminal route, your dreams will either seem unattainable or will likely lead you down the wrong path. representation does not mean that one is better than the other, but it acknowledges the differences.

i represent.

november 10
“momma ain't strong enough to raise no boy, what's his father name?”
Meet The Parents
The Blueprint 2: The Gift & The Curse

how were you created? it took a mother and a father to create you. in accordance with god, a human life cannot be created without the participation of both man and woman. therefore, both should reap the blessings and responsibilities associated with raising that life. there are things that are taught by a mother that a father cannot teach and vice versa. everyone has been assigned a role and it is up to us to play our position, not allow situations that are within our control to interfere with the growth and development of the seeds we’ve planted. your mark on this world may very well be in the person that your raise. don’t let your bad choices result in the abandonment and ultimate emotional destruction of a being that did not request to be put on this earth. do your part, whether it be to teach a child to love or hunt. understand that they need to know how to do both. now, that’s balance.

i take care of my responsibilities.

november 11
"but when you live by the gun you die by the same fate."
Meet The Parents
The Blueprint 2: The Gift & The Curse

often people dish it out but can never fathom being the recipient of the actions that they so freely subject others to. whether it be niceness or nastiness. you get from the world what you put into the world. what are your thoughts? what are your words? what are your actions? what is in your heart? there are no cheat codes. it will all eventually even out and catch up to you. love is so powerful, and it's so easy to project. all you have to do is treat others how you hope to be treated. why not practice love?

i am living a life of love.

november 12
"put this shit in motion ain't no rewinding me back."
U Don't Know
The Blueprint 2: The Gift & The Curse

do you start what you finish? or somewhere along the path do you lose the excitement, passion and confidence that you had at the beginning? why is that? did the momentum slow down? stop talking yourself out of your dreams! stop getting your own way! stop preventing your own achievements! if this sounds like you, you might be your own biggest hater. you're supposed to be your biggest fan. your biggest cheerleader. your own coach and your best player. press play! follow your plans! see them through to the end and keep allowing yourself to get bigger and better. don't start and stop. that fucks up the flow and make for a very bumpy ride.

i finish what i start.

november 13
“momma ain't raise no fool. put me anywhere on god's green earth, i'll triple my worth.”
U Don't Know
The Blueprint 2: The Gift & The Curse

have you seen neighborhoods undergo gentrification? do you notice how an area that once looked like an eye sore, blossomed into something beautiful? how’s that? have you witnessed buildings be abandoned for decades only to have someone purchase it and open a market or something better? and you wonder, how did this person manage to do what no one else managed to do over decades. create the things you wish existed. you can’t just wish for them; you have to work for them to make it happen. sometimes, the circumstances force you to get creative. if you find an opportunity to earn that costs $5 and you only have $1, then you have to find 4 other people with $1 and work together to turn your $5 to $15. you can’t allow yourself to be defeated. use your intellect. use your creativity. use your network and make those things work for you.

i am smart enough to find my way.

november 14
“was born to dictate, never follow orders.”
U Don't Know
The Blueprint 2: The Gift & The Curse

there’s leaders and their followers. which one are you? do you make the rules or follow the rules? or are you someone that breaks the rules until you’re caught and forced to follow even harsher rules? instead of rebelling and breaking the rules, why not do what needs to be done to rewrite the rules in your favor? prisons are currently populated in significant number by marijuana offenders, now states across the country are legalizing the use and sale of cannabis. how’s that? because those that recognized how lucrative the industry is are doing the work to change the law. remember prohibition? remember slavery? don’t allow others to make the rules, it up to you to change the game.

it is what i say it is in my life.

november 15
“i tell you the difference between me and them. they tryna get they ones, i'm tryna get them m's.”
U Don't Know
The Blueprint 2: The Gift & The Curse

think big. bigger. even bigger. remember when being a millionaire was as big as we could dream. now, we’re dreaming billionaire dreams. how about dreaming in the trillions? you are the only one that can impose your limits. who gon’ stop you, huh? others can try to tell you what you can’t do, but it is up to you to prove them wrong. they’re only in control of what they can and can’t do. not you! be led by your dreams. do not allow yourself to be confined by others’ cages. set yourself apart. find a circle that inspires you to think bigger and conspires with you to be better. show the naysayers that it can be done if you think different and inspire them to do more.

my goals separate and elevate me.

november 16
“world can't hold me, too much ambition, always knew it’d be like this when i was in the kitchen.”
On To The Next
The Blueprint 3

what do you aspire to be? what do you dream about? are you doing it now or do you sit at the job that pays you thinking about what you really want to be doing? what are you inspired by? do your dreams motivate you to work harder? do they guide you to make better choices? do they make you jump out of bed in the morning eager to get a step closer to the things you want out of life? how hard are you working? or are you just doing the bare minimum? are you hopeful or are you defeated? don’t settle for the life you have, because when you settle you get stuck! keep moving, as long as you’re moving in the direction of your goals.

i go after the things i want.

november 17
"i'd get more in depth, if you boys really real enough."
Run This Town
The Blueprint 3

how many people do you really know? do you have lots of acquaintances or have you taken the time to get to know people and their stories. their values. their beliefs. their likes and dislikes. their hopes and dreams. their fears. their strengths and weaknesses. again, how many people do you know? the number is probably a lot fewer than when you initially answered, right? now ask yourself, why haven't you made deeper connections with more people? are you willing to make yourself vulnerable to share your story? are you too judgmental? do you have real conversations? or is it just that you don't care? sometimes, peoples' stories are so deep that it can arouse emotions within you that you may not be ready or willing to deal with. often, people ask questions although they aren't ready for honest answers. others ask questions and don't care to hear the answers. when was the last time you asked someone how they were doing? did you listen for an authentic response?

i can handle the truth!

november 18
"i'll tighten my belt before i beg for help."
Justify My Thug
The Black Album

when tough times arise, how do you survive? do you begin making concessions and get creative or do you hold your hand out? seriously, do you hold your hand out? i used to think that was just a saying until, one day, i saw an able-bodied, seemingly sane adult man extend his hand and ask for money as i left the grocery store. he didn't offer to carry my groceries or wash my windows in exchange for some cash. he extended his hand and asked for money. i was baffled. i'd seen people with cups, buckets, squeegees and everything in between. but this my first experience with an adult that had their hand out. it seemed so natural to him. it made me wonder about his story. what, if any, attempts had he made before he got to this point? what sacrifices are you willing to make?

i sacrifice to get the things i want.

november 19
"oh yeah i'm rare, i'm aware that i'm rare."
Real As It Gets
The Blueprint 3

you are one of one. there is no one like you and there will be no one like you. only if you allow yourself to be exactly who you are. the things you're attracted to, interested in, passionate about, good at are not random. the family you were born to, the city you were born in, the neighborhood you grew up in, the people you befriend and unfriend. none of it is accidental. all of these things conspire to make you who you are and propel you to who you're meant to become. don't take these people, places or things for granted. some of them will be sunshine and others will be rain. they're both needed to allow you to grow and come into your own. take pride in that and confidently make your mark.

there is no one like me.

november 20
“blueprints for sale. following my footprints, you can't fail.”
Real As It Gets
The Blueprint 3

who are your mentors? your o.g.’s? what biographies and autobiographies are you reading and watching? who’s moves are you watching? what are you learning from the successes and failures of people that have ascended to a level that you aspire to? are you taking notes, or do you think these people are here for your entertainment only? of course, some mistakes have to be made in order to fully appreciate the lesson, but lots of missteps can be avoided if you follow the footsteps of the people that came before you. if they’ve already paved the way, why would you waste your time and energy shoveling? you can pick up where they left off and take things even further and be an example to the ones watching you.

i leave a clear path for those that come after.

november 21
"nigga, respect the game. that should be it."
Heart Of The City (Ain't No Love)
The Blueprint

its rules in any business. there are also people that refuse to follow the rules. i think we all can agree that there are some rules that just don't make sense and need to be broken, but there are rules that lay the groundwork and maintain order, decency and honor. regardless of the industry one rule that's transferable is no hating and no copying. instead of using energy to hate on someone else, you should redirect that into your own endeavors in the hopes of a better outcome. stealing someone's else's concept is also dishonorable. while it is expected to be inspired by another's work, it is a quite different than completely duplicating someone else's ideas. what's for you is for you and what's for them is for them. stay in your own lane and go at your own pace to limit the probability of a crash.

i keep my eyes on my own paper.

november 22
"if i can't live by my word then i'd much rather die."
Thank You
The Blueprint 3

how thoughtful are you with the words that you speak? do you mean what you say? do you speak in truth? do you speak in love or hate? take some time to consider this. when you're angry do you say things you don't mean? when you're excited or happy do you make promises you don't keep? do you say things about others that are untrue? do you claim to have done things you've never done and to have seen places you've only seen in pictures? all of these factors count and contribute to the determination as to whether your word is your bond. i'm sure you've been told in your life that if you have anything nice to say, then don't say anything at all. it's not nice to say things that aren't true. keep it real. be reliable. be a good source of information. say what you mean. mean what you say.

my word is my bond.

november 23
"i'm cut from a different cloth, i'm just who the shoe fits."
Thank You
The Blueprint 3

you are you and that is your power. no one else can be you. they can try, but all the things that have conspired to create the person that you are and will become are uniquely you. have you ever met someone that has lived your exact live? nope. have you ever me someone that is affected by or responds to every single situation exactly as you have or would? nope. it won't happen. you are one of one and no one can fill your shoes in your absence. your steps, your footprints are uniquely you. have faith in that. be confident in who you are and who you will become. stop worrying about who will come after you. just make sure you set the bar. make your mark. be a hard act to follow. be so good that you can't be ignored or forgotten. inspire others to be great in their efforts to fill your shoes.

i am unique.

november 24
"beautiful music when champagne flutes click."
Thank You
The Blueprint 3

life consists of wins and lessons. you've got to celebrate the wins and allow the lessons to make you better. in fact, a lesson that makes you better is also a valid reason to celebrate. while you may think that the lesson is really a loss and you may be tempted to write it off as a painful memory, i urge you to toast to your lessons with a glass of champagne as you would toast to a new year. be hopeful because you've been tested and strengthen by challenging times. see the opportunities presented in your trials. opportunities for growth are certainly cause for celebration if you recognize them and take advantage of them. become better with each endeavor. make some things happen. make some people better. turn your pain into champagne.

i celebrate the good in things.

november 25
"niggas want my old shit, buy my old album
niggas stuck on stupid, i gotta keep it moving."
On To The Next
The Blueprint 3

change is natural and growth is imperative. if you're not growing, you're not living. you have two options, grow or deteriorate. change will happen regardless, although some will try to resist it. people will constantly bring up the past in an effort to resist growth or avoid certain experiences and lessons to stunt growth in the hopes of staying in their comfort zone. nothing great comes from comfort zones. you have to push your boundaries, try new things, meet new people, learn new lessons and allow the path to guide you toward your goals. each day be better than the day prior. allow yourself to grow freely and see where it takes you. if people don't approve of your growth and want to confine you to your past, accept that you've outgrown them. be content with your memories and move graciously towards your future. level up.

i am growing.

november 26
"i moved onward, the only direction."
On To The Next
The Blueprint 3

your goal is ahead of you. keep going. even if you're only taking baby steps, be confident that you are moving in the right direction. don't spend too much time looking in your rearview. use the past as a reference and use the lessons you've accumulated to help guide you. open new doors and go after what you want. believe in your potential for greatness and be motivated by your faith. where do you see yourself in 1 year? 3 years? 5 years? 20 years? i'm sure your plans are big! what is coming will be better than what has gone, so what are you waiting for? let go of the past and leap into your future. put in the work and keep believing. trust that it will all work out as it should if you do your part.

i'm looking forward to reaching my goals.

november 27
"all i need is a partner to play spades with the cards up, all trust."
Excuse Me Miss
The Blueprint 2: The Gift And The Curse

trusting someone can be greater than loving them. trust is built on consistency in actions; therefore, it is a bond that is earned. love is often unexplained. trust is the foundation of most relationships as it allows for effective communication. who do you trust? who do you allow yourself to be vulnerable with? who do you sleep next to? if you have to sleep with one eye open, it's safe to say you don't trust them. so, you have to wonder, why are you sleeping with them? who are you intimate with? this act can literally end a life or create one. so, having sex with random people that you don't trust could be perceived as a reckless mishandling of your life. make sure the person you've teamed up with has your back the way you have theirs and you both are working towards building with each other instead of working against one other. be as picky with the selection of your mate as you are with your spades partner. don't make your relationship like a game of poker.

i trust my partner.

november 28
"said it ain't where you from yo it's where you at."
All Around The World
The Blueprint 2: The Gift And The Curse

humble beginnings build character. They stimulate your creativity and strengthen your spirit. It's up to you to make use those things to take you where you want to go. Can you make a meal from a refrigerator that is seemingly empty? Can you make $100 last for weeks? If you know how to survive when you have nothing, you are less rattled by challenging times than someone who has otherwise had a comfortable life. Your will to succeed may also be stronger because you want the tough times of your past to stay in the past. use the lessons learned and skills acquired from your past to fuel your elevation. How far have you come? How much have you grown? you can't control where you start, but where you finish is one hundred percent up to you.

i am responsible for my own growth.

november 29

"i put my hand on my heart, that means i feel you. real recognize real and you looking familiar."

All Around The World

The Blueprint 2: The Gift And The Curse

have you ever met someone and connected with them immediately? something about them seemed to speak to you. the things they talk about. the things that interest them. the things that disinterest them. the things they value. their morals. you're drawn to them and they too, are drawn to you. take note of these righteous people. value them. keep them close. understand that real is rare. that's not just a sound bite, that's the truth. if you are a genuine person, lots of people will be attracted to you and try to absorb your good energy. how can you detect the real from the fake? pay attention to whether you feel charged or drained in their presence. are you spending time deciphering their words and actions or do they seem to be transparent? seek out the people that stimulate you.

i've got a thing for genuine people.

november 30
"you can't change a player's game in the ninth inning."
Ain't No Nigga
Reasonable Doubt

i'm sure you've heard that you can't teach an old dog new tricks. people tend to do what they've always done. it's difficult to change habits, so we become what we repeatedly do. if you run every day, you are a runner. it would be surprising if you one day decided to start cycling. it takes tremendous effort to change habits, whether they are bad or good. think about the last time you tried to change something about yourself. did you try to wake up earlier every day? did you try to eat healthier? did you try to save money? i'm sure it was difficult to change your behavior. so, imagine how hard it must be to change someone else's behavior. not only does redirection require intense focus and discipline, but you must also first be motivated to make the change. the decision to change habits and behaviors comes from within. your mind must be open to the change of behavior and you have to act accordingly. if you are looking for a different outcome, make the choice to do something different.

i am what i repeatedly do.

december 1
"cure the Black man and bring him back to the way he was in his original state."
the originators
To Your Soul (Jaz O)

if you do a little research, it's easy to find out the tragedies and triumphs of those that came before you. history is to be used as a reference for you to build upon the strengths, avoid the mistakes, and find opportunities for improvement. There is an African proverb that says, "until the lion tells his side of the story, the tale will always glorify the hunter." do you benefit from the blood, sweat and tears of those that came before you without valuing their sacrifice? what are you doing to ensure that their suffering and hard work are recognized and respected for generations to come and will never erased? or will you participate in their removal from the history books? it's easy to rewrite history if no one is looking. it's what you do every time you throw away pictures from your past relationships. if no one contests it, it's like it didn't happen. when you're 90, you can tell your great-great grandchildren that your husband was the only man you'd ever loved. that's one of the benefits of social media. once you put it out there, it's out there.

i am on the right side of history.

december 2
"once you start, you can't stop it."
Show & Prove (Big Daddy Kane)

how many tabs are open on your computer? how many to-do lists do you have with unfinished tasks? set your goals and don't stop until you accomplish them. if something is worth starting, why not see it through all the way to the end. it's like watching a movie. sometimes you have to finish it in the hopes that it'll turn out differently than you're expecting and even better than you hoped it would when you started. you also owe it to yourself to not be a quitter. no matter what you convince yourself of, if you never finish anything, you're a quitter. in order to win, you can't quit and the easiest way to lose is to quit.

i will finish what i start.

december 3
"but i hate when a nigga sit back admiring yours. young blood you betta get that."
Medley: Intro / A Million
In My Lifetime Vol 1

are you inspired by others to attain your goals? do they inspire you to the point of action? or do you just sit back dreaming about the things others have and have accomplished without formulating a plan of how to get up and get your own? the difference in how you respond to others success is a huge indicator as to whether you a dreamer or a doer. a hater or congratulator. a foe or a friend. a player or a fan. don't just sit back watching others do, do for yourself. if they can live their dreams, so can you. be inspired by others and do something every day to ensure that you too will one day have what you desire. the very action of getting up every day and trying is admirable.

i will make my dreams a reality.

december 4
“i'm tryna make all of my dreams materialize.”
In My Lifetime
Streets Is Watching

there is a saying that nothing comes to a sleeper but a dream. so, if you want to turn your dreams into reality you have to wake up and make it happen. dreams don’t miraculously come true. this isn’t a fairytale. put your plan to work and believe that you have what it takes to live your dreams. why else would you have been given that dream? there are billions of people in the world that all have dreams. yours belongs to you. if you can dream it, you can achieve it, but you must first have the courage to pursue it. dream in detail so it will be easier for you to stay on track and identify when you’re heading in the right direction

i am creating my future.

december 5
"let me be great."
F.U.T.W.
Magna Carta... Holy Grail

on the path to greatness, you will have to overcome some opposition. it won't be easy because of the magnitude of your mission. if it were easy, everyone would be doing it, and no one would value it. we all have the potential for greatness, but the willingness to remain focused and not be discouraged or defeated by challenges is crucial. consistently work your plan one step at a time and resist the temptation to play it safe and perform in mediocrity. you don't need anyone else's permission to be great. you were built for this. ignore the noise from the people in the stands and stay away from bad vibes. go towards your greatness.

the universe is aligning for me to be my best.

december 6
“don't get caught perpetrating the cool ones all around the world.”
Hawaiian Sophie (Jaz O)

there is no one like you and there will never be another. so why would you want to try to be anyone else but yourself? be inspired by the things that attract you but don’t try to duplicate them. nothing is ever as good as the original. you’ve got to do what feels right to you, fuck what people think. why do you assign importance to their opinion in your life? just do you. embrace your individuality. be confident in yourself. following the crowd is easy, but it takes courage to do your own thing. your power is in being exactly who you are, so understand what makes you unique and put that out into the world. the world doesn’t need any more copycats. it needs you.

nobody can do me better than me.

december 7
"i found a new route, you 'bout to see my life change."
In My Lifetime
Streets Is Watching

have you ever felt like you were stuck in a rut? it's probably because you were still living in the past. have you ever had the courage to leave a job that you hated? end a relationship that made you unhappy? change your diet? change your spending habits? after living your life a certain way for so long it can be easy to do the things you've always done despite constantly getting disappointing outcomes. einstein is famously credited for defining insanity as expecting different results although your behavior hasn't changed. in hindsight, that is obviously an unrealistic expectation. however, hindsight is twenty-twenty. if you ever find yourself stuck, look at what you've been doing to get unstuck. your goals are waiting for you.

i do something different to get a different outcome.

december 8
"i know the price, know the risks. know the wrongs and the rights"
In My Lifetime
Streets Is Watching

think. think before you speak. think before you act. do you seriously consider the possible outcomes in response to your words and your actions? or do you not know what you're going to say until you hear it come out of your mouth? do you just do what feels right at the moment without having considered the risk associated with it? for every curse there is an echo. for every action, there is a reaction. you're always one decision away from a different life. therefore, don't let a moment in time in which you're angry or careless put your plan for your life at jeopardy. don't allow other people to make decisions that will affect your life without you having weighed in on it. you get the final say. don't say things in anger or lust that you won't be able to take back. be thoughtful and intentional with your words and actions and make sure that what you're thinking matches what you're saying and what you 're saying matches what you're doing. it's your life. you're in control. the stakes are high.

i consider risks versus rewards.

december 9
“is this world my world? am i the star of stars?”
In My Lifetime
Streets Is Watching

the world is yours. act like it. take care of it and it will take care of you. understand that your life is yours and you owe it to yourself and the creator to shine during your time. use your gifts. make the best use of your ”15 minutes” and really put on a show. the world is your stage. there is no time for stage fright. do the things you dream about. do the things you speak about. before you know it, it’ll be over, and it’ll be time to remind the world of all that you’ve accomplished. what will your obituary say? don’t spend your life thinking “what if?”, let your mantra be “what next?”

i am the star of my life.

december 10
"uhh, from the beginning, see, we never seen the ending."
In My Lifetime
In My Lifetime Vol 1

we've heard it our whole lives ... just do it. if you know in your heart that you want better, that there is another level for you, or that what is coming is better than what has passed then it is up to you to act and make it happen. even if you haven't figured out the plan in its entirety, just take the first step. don't spend so much time overthinking that you end up stuck doing nothing and never give yourself a fair shot. don't limit your potential, act on it. what would you do if you knew you couldn't fail? shoot your shot and act on the things that inspire you. proceed as if you already know that it is impossible for you to fail.

i will take the first step.

december 11
"and niggas don't be mad cause it's all about progression. loiterers should be arrested."
On To The Next One
The Blueprint 3

stop standing in place. life is about change. change involves growth. make sure you're being inspired to change for the better. if you're not growing, then what are you doing? have you not learned anything? have you not been anywhere? have you not experienced anything? have you not met any interesting people? what are you building and who are you building with? tear down those old ways of thinking and working that left you stagnant. step out of your comfort zone and find a new normal to experience new levels of success in other areas of your life. how have you changed over the years? how have you progressed? how far have you come? think about you will improve in the coming years based on the things you're working on today. how far are you willing to go?

i am continuously evolving.

december 12
“so, with or without any of y'all involvement, we coming for all of this, respect my conglomerate.”
So Ambitious
The Blueprint 3

only you can change your life, no one can do it for you. there will always be people that have no interest in involving themselves in your plan for various reasons. they may not believe in the plan, they may not believe in you, they may not believe in themselves, they may want to wait and see how it turns out. those folks are very easy to weed out early. forget them. those aren’t your people. everyone won’t be a part of your journey. you’ll have no problem identifying the people that believe in you, support you and want to work with you. these are the people that see your magic. these people understand your vision. these people deserve to be a part of it. it’s quite easy, they’re either with you or against you. but first, you need to make sure your confidence in yourself and your vision is unwavering. go for what is yours.

i am going after my goals.

december 13
"i went from pauper to the president, cause every deal i ever made set precedent, niggas probably thought i'd fall without old buddy, oh buddy, what i do is make more money."
So Ambitious
The Blueprint 3

everyone isn't meant to go all the way on your journey. after all, it is your journey. there are times when you'll be aligned, and you'll be able to make moves together that are mutually beneficial and make memories for the history books. but don't ever allow yourself to be held down or held back by someone that is stagnant. don't allow yourself to be derailed by another's detour. keep going. if it's meant to be, they'll catch up to you. you've got things to do, days to seize, growth to make and records to break. you're the author of your story, the characters may change with each chapter, that doesn't mean they didn't make an impression. the ending is up to you.

i am responsible for my rise.

december 14
“leave a mark that can't erase, neither space nor time.”
Young Forever
The Blueprint 3

how do you want to be remembered? what have you accomplished? what are you doing? are you just sitting back watching others get things done and make shit happen? don’t give up or give in to things that you know are wrong. take a stance. make a difference. study history and you’ll realize that everyone that actually made it to the history books set out to make a difference, not history. don’t do it for the fame, fame is fleeting. make a difference in people’s lives and you’ll always be remembered. those that you’ve impacted will spread the word. use your time wisely.

i am making history.

december 15
"i'm not afraid of dying, i'm afraid of not trying."
Beach Chair
Kingdom Come

fear can be crippling. the fear of failure and fear of death are at the top of the list of common things many people are afraid of. death is life's only guarantee, so there is no point in worrying about it. your worry will not change the outcome, so why fear what you can't change. when it's over, it's over and you won't have to worry about it anymore. fear can sometimes be enough to make people not pursue their dreams and all they're left with regrets and thoughts of woulda, coulda, shoulda and what if. try to face your fears in an effort to change your circumstances. the fear that you feel is not real; it's all in your mind. it's a test to see if you really want what you say you want. if you don't try, you've already failed, so just do it and consider the possibility that you might fly. remember what we were all taught as children: if at first you don't succeed... try, try, again.

i will try my best to do my best.

december 16
“every day, hit every wave like i’m hawaiian.”
Beach Chair
Kingdom Come

life is like the ocean and the waves will come and go and some will be bigger and more forceful than others. you can’t stop them, so you best learn to surf. sometimes you’ll provide the wave, other times you’ll be riding them. there will be highs and lows, ups and downs, wins and lessons, good times and bad. there may be times when you get knocked off your board and it’s up to you whether you sink or swim. remember, it’s not what happens to you that matters, but it is how you respond to it and what you get out of those things that count in the end. keep going. everything that happens in life is an opportunity for you to improve yourself, so roll with the punches and punch back. don’t ever give up.

i’m living my best life.

december 17
"no compass comes with this life just eyes."
Beach Chair
Kingdom Come

unfortunately, life doesn't come with an instruction book. your life is in your hands. it is up to you to make smart moves along your journey. don't fall asleep at the wheel. pay attention. tap into your natural instincts. be aware of your surroundings. feel the vibes. listen closely. who are you surrounded by? what are they teaching you? what are you reading? what mistakes are you making? are you learning from them? in your life, you'll realize that there are no rights or wrongs. even the things that may seem as if they may have been wrong are only opportunities to learn and sharpen yourself. make sure you're thinking before you act, but don't get stuck overthinking. don't beat yourself up too much for your missteps. just adjust and keep living.

i have all that i need to make this a great life.

december 18
"nobody built like you, you designed yourself."
A Dream
The Blueprint 2: The Gift And The Curse

take a look around. notice all the different shapes, sizes of the people around you. notice the skin tones, tones of voice, different hair textures and even different smells. now take another look and pay attention to the people around you that are dressed in the same style, manipulating their natural hair in the same styles just to fit in. do you know how much science went into creating you? science did its part so now it's up to you to do yours. why fit in when you were made to stand out? how else can you explain having siblings with the same mom and dad and not looking and acting exactly alike? you're attracted do different things. you excel in different things. you are unique. do you.

i'm one of one.

december 19
"they say a midget standing on the giant's shoulder can see much further than the giant."
Hovi Baby
The Blueprint 2: The Gift And The Curse

as the underdog, there will certainly be things that you're unable to do as effectively as you like alone. you might lack the funding, expertise or muscle. learn from those that came before you. learn from those doing better than you. the writings are on the wall. do your research. if you want to be great, do what great people have learn from and replicate what has already been tried, tested and proven. you don't have to reinvent the wheel, if it has already been done. copy, paste, improve. giants built the pyramids, so what are you capable of?

i benefit from the lessons passed on from my ancestors.

december 20
"i got now, i don't care who got next."
Hovi Baby
The Blueprint 2: The Gift & The Curse

the clock is ticking. everyone will have their time, it's up to you what you do with it. will you make your time count, or will you just waste your time watching the clock or scrolling your timeline looking at what everyone else is doing? it is up to you to be fully present and leverage the time that you have. the stage is yours, for now, so put on a show. you cannot waste your time worrying about what the person who's coming after you will do with his time or what the person who came before you did. pick up where the ones before you left off and set the bar for those that will most certainly come after you. make sure to set the bar high to ensure that you will not easily be forgotten.

my time is now.

december 21
"the world is mine and can't nobody keep it from me."
The Watcher 2
The Blueprint 2: The Gift And The Curse

the world is yours, so do what you've been put here to do. don't let others interfere with you accomplishing the things you've decided you wanted for your life. don't allow yourself to be sidetracked by friends, family and foes or be shut down and shut out by gatekeepers and haters. people will have their own agenda and their agenda may not be aligned with yours and may, therefore, have the potential to interfere with your plans and leave you feeling unfulfilled. you get what you focus on. it is up to you to choose to be focused on your goals or to choose your distractions. it's your life, it's your world and the choice is yours.

i cannot be stopped.

december 22
"soon you gon' see you can't replace him
with cheap imitations for these generations."
Encore
The Black Album

nobody can do you like you. if you do what comes natural to you and what you're passionate about, it'll be impossible to duplicate. people will mock you, smile anyway. people will hate you, show love anyway. people will copy you, be flattered. when you are doing you, you are not replaceable. no one can do you like you. with that knowledge, know that there are no wrongs in your life. everything you do will be intended to point you in the right direction by force or by faith. believe in yourself, be clear on who you are, know the light you shine and never allow anyone to dim your light or steal your shine.

i am one of one.

december 23
"put us together--how they gon' stop both us? whatever she lacks, i'm right over her shoulder when i'm off track, mami is keeping' me focused."
'03 bonnie & Clyde
The Blueprint²: The Gift And The Curse

do you play your position? in any relationship, platonic, professional, or otherwise each person must play their role to allow the relationship to bloom and reach its potential. what are your weaknesses? what are your strengths? where is there opportunity for growth? what holes are in your relationship that may create a threat or make either person replaceable. take a close inventory at your personal and professional relationships and make sure that you are maximizing them and not taking the people and the relationship for granted by doing the bare minimum. make others better and allow yourself to be made better by the people that you pair up with.

i'm surrounded by people that compliment me.

december 24
"the problem is you dudes treat the one that you loving' with the same respect that you treat the one that you humping."
03 bonnie & Clyde
The Blueprint²: The Gift And The Curse

loving relationships not only have titles, but they have expectations that come with those titles. generally, there is an expectation of exclusivity and if not, there is this expectation that your significant other is put on a pedestal and shown a level of respect and loyalty unparalleled to any other person. so why do so many relationships end disastrously? often, it seems that we take for granted why we chose our partner and why they chose us. they showed you something different, something better than you'd ever experienced with other flings and were worth you committing your best to them. i love you is not just a statement that you make. when you say i love you it should be your reminder and reaffirming to stay committed, stay in agreement, and operate in loyalty, honesty and respect.

i will not confuse the importance of the players in the game.

december 25
"can't be scared to fail, search and perfection."
On To The Next
The Blueprint 3

do you stand on the wall at parties because you're nervous you'll be judged for not having dance moves? don't let the fear of failure or the pursuit of perfection stop you from trying at all. do you! even if things don't work out how you planned, you'll learn some valuable lessons and have some great experiences. fail forward. no one is perfect, but you can certainly get up each day and put in work. in fact, put more work in than you did the day before and you're sure to ultimately achieve your best. nothing beats a failure but a try.

i am pursuing excellence.

december 26
“nigga, i get my "by any means" on whenever there's a drought. get your umbrellas out because that's when i brainstorm.”
Interlude Public Service Announcement
The Black Album

out of necessity comes opportunity. have you ever eaten a butter sandwich? sugar sandwiches? you may have if there may have been days when your refrigerator and cupboards were bare. and guess what, as curious as those dishes sound, they were actually surprisingly good. if your fridge was full, you would’ve never thought to make such a thing. think about all of the inventions of enslaved people in an attempt to alleviate the strain on their lives. what do you do when your back is against the wall? do you fold or do you get creative and do what needs to be done? do you explore the possibilities, or do you give up? don’t be disheartened by hard times. remember that you’ve got heart.

i cannot be stopped.

december 27
"when you first come in the game, they try to play you. then you drop a couple of hits, look how they wave to you."
Encore
The Black Album

do you remember your first day of high school? how about the last day? the way people treated you on those two days was very different, wasn't it? for some reason, it is hard to get the support of others early on, but once you've proven yourself everyone acts like they've been rooting for you from the beginning. don't let that discourage you from working hard and attaining your goals, you don't need a fan club. take notes of who overlooked you but welcome them when they are sweating you. deal with them accordingly. don't take it personal, people have trouble believing in themselves, so don't expect everyone to believe in you.

i believe in me.

december 28
"and, no, i ain't perfect; nobody walking' this earth's surface is."
03 bonnie & Clyde
The Blueprint[2]: The Gift And The Curse

you are a work in progress. none of us is perfect. however, it is possible to find someone that is perfect for you. the things that another might find intolerable might suit you just fine. your ex-girl might've thought you were boring because you didn't enjoy nightclubs and being around crowds, and now you've found someone that is boring too. you may have been criticized for being too flashy by your old crew, now you've linked up with your own destiny's children. your last boyfriend may have talked down to you because you couldn't cook, but your new boyfriend is a chef. don't force things that don't fit and don't stick with people that are merely tolerating you. pay close attention to when who you are is complemented by who they are and also, where your strengths match their weakness and vice versa. surround yourself with those that are perfect for you.

i am a work in progress.

december 29
"as fate would have it, jay's status appears to be at an all-time high, perfect time to say goodbye."
Encore
The Black Album

how does it make you feel to be known? how does it make you feel when you've accomplished something? sometimes, people get caught up chasing that feeling and expect it without doing the work. they just stand there basking in the spotlight without considering that they might one day, be booed off the stage. if you want to stay on top, you must stay competitive. you have to pursue things and empower people that keep you elevated. what have you done lately? or are you still living in the past? who have you empowered? what's your team look like? or are you only focused on yourself and your success? focus on the big picture and know when it's time to pass the baton and merge into another lane. don't get forced out because of your ego. know when it's time to make your exit. don't be the 50-year-old in a night club full of the new wave of fake i.d.'s.

i go out on top.

december 30
"lord we know who we are, yet we know not what we may be."
Marcy Me
4:44

you can't know where you're going until you know where you come from. you originate from greatness. look at all that's been accomplished by your ancestors with so little. with so many challenges. with so many adversaries. you are the child of survivors. you are equipped with the strength to help you realize your dreams and accomplish your mission. whenever you want to give up, just think of how far you've come and how far you have the possibility to go... then go further. you've got this. fulfill your potential.

i shoot for the moon.

december 31
"grand opening, grand closing."
Encore
The Black Album

do you show up fashionably late to allow yourself an opportunity to make an entrance to get the attention you want? many people show up and show off and sneak out of the door, so they aren't missed. why not leave with the same good energy you brought with you? solidify your impact in people's hearts and memories. if no one misses you when you're gone did you really show us what you've got? your arrival on this earth was a special occasion and your departure will be the same. make sure you make the time in between just as exciting. live everyday as if it is your last. what did you do today? what did you do yesterday? would you be satisfied with what you've accomplished if today were your last day? think about the momentum that you kick of the new year with. new year's resolutions? what did you resolve? did you accomplish what you set out to do? why or why not? stay encouraged. stay motivated. stay focused on the things you want. stay clear on how you want to be remembered.

i will leave the world how i came, with a splash.

"thank you, thank you, thank you
please hold your applause
for i just applied logic keys
keys open doors"
JAY-Z
Thank You
The Blueprint 3

references

Jaz O. Hawaiian Sophie, *To Your Soul*. EMI USA, 1990.

Jay-Z. Broken English & Drug Sellin, *Demo*. 1993.

Big Daddy Kane. Show & Prove (feat. Jay-Z), *Daddy's Home*. MCA Records, 1994.

Jay-Z. Can I Live, *Reasonable Doubt*. Roc-A-Fella/Priority Records, 1996.

_____. Brooklyn's Finest, *Reasonable Doubt*. Roc-A-Fella/Priority Records, 1996.

_____. Politics as Usual, *Reasonable Doubt*. Roc-A-Fella/Priority Records, 1996.

_____. Regrets, *Reasonable Doubt*. Roc-A-Fella/Priority Records, 1996.

_____. 22 Two's, *Reasonable Doubt*. Roc-A-Fella/Priority Records, 1996.

_____. Show Me What You Got, *Reasonable Doubt*. Roc-A-Fella/Priority Records, 1996.

_____. Can I Live II, *Reasonable Doubt*. Roc-A-Fella/Priority Records, 1996.

_____. D'evils, *Reasonable Doubt*. Roc-A-Fella/Priority Records, 1996.

_____. Feelin' It, *Reasonable Doubt*. Roc-A-Fella/Priority Records, 1996.

_____. Dead Presidents, *Reasonable Doubt*. Roc-A-Fella/Priority Records, 1996.

_____. Friend or Foe, *Reasonable Doubt*. Roc-A-Fella/Priority Records, 1996.

_____. Lucky Me, *Reasonable Doubt*. Roc-A-Fella/Priority Records, 1996.

_____. Can't Knock the Hustle, *Reasonable Doubt*. Roc-A-Fella/Priority Records, 1996.

_____. Ain't No Nigga, *Reasonable Doubt*. Roc-A-Fella/Priority Records, 1996.

_____. Lucky Me, *In My Lifetime Vol. 1*. Roc-A-Fella/Def Jam, 1997.

_____. Real Niggaz, *In My Lifetime Vol. 1*. Roc-A-Fella/Def Jam, 1997.

_____. Coming of Age, *In My Lifetime Vol. 1*. Roc-A-Fella/Def Jam, 1997.

_____. Where I'm From, *In My Lifetime Vol. 1*. Roc-A-Fella/Def Jam, 1997.

_____. Medley: Intro/A Million, *In My Lifetime Vol. 1*. Roc-A-Fella/Def Jam, 1997.

_____. Hard Knock Life, *Vol. 2...Hard Knock Life*. Roc-A-Fella/Def Jam, 1998.

_____. If I Should Die, *Vol. 2...Hard Knock Life*. Roc-A-Fella/Def Jam, 1998.

_____. You're Only A Customer, *Streets Is Watching Soundtrack*. Roc-A-Fella/Def Jam, 1998.

_____. In My Lifetime, *Streets Is Watching Soundtrack*. Roc-A-Fella/Def Jam, 1998.

DJ Clue. Gangsta Shit (feat. Jay-Z), *The Professional*. Desert Storm/R0c-A-Fella/Def Jams, 1998.

Beanie Sigel. Anything (feat. Jay-Z), *The Truth*. Roc-A-Fella/Def Jams, 2000.

Jay-Z. Takeover, *The Blueprint*. Roc-A-Fella/Def Jam, 2001.

_____. Never Change, *The Blueprint*. Roc-A-Fella/Def Jam, 2001.

_____. Heart of the City (Ain't No Love) , *The Blueprint*. Roc-A-Fella/Def Jam, 2001.

_____. Renegade, *The Blueprint*. Roc-A-Fella/Def Jam, 2001.

_____. Song Cry, *The Blueprint*. Roc-A-Fella/Def Jam, 2001.

_____. Hola Hovito, *The Blueprint*. Roc-A-Fella/Def Jam, 2001.

_____. Lyrical Exercise, *The Blueprint*. Roc-A-Fella/Def Jam, 2001.

_____. U Don't Know, *The Blueprint*. Roc-A-Fella/Def Jam, 2001.

_____. The Ruler's Back, *The Blueprint*. Roc-A-Fella/Def Jam, 2001.

_____. Izzo, *The Blueprint*. Roc-A-Fella/Def Jam, 2001.

_____. Girls, Girls, Girls, *The Blueprint*. Roc-A-Fella/Def Jam, 2001.

_____. Jigga That Nigga, *The Blueprint*. Roc-A-Fella/Def Jam, 2001.

_____. Girls, Girls, Girls, (Part 2) , *The Blueprint*. Roc-A-Fella/Def Jam, 2001.

_____. A Dream, *The Blueprint2: The Gift & The Curse*. Roc-A-Fella/Def Jams, 2002.

_____. Blueprint 2, *The Blueprint2: The Gift & The Curse*. Roc-A-Fella/Def Jams, 2002.

_____. Hovi Baby, *The Blueprint2: The Gift & The Curse*. Roc-A-Fella/Def Jams, 2002.

_____. Guns & Roses, *The Blueprint2: The Gift & The Curse*. Roc-A-Fella/Def Jams, 2002.

_____. Nigga Please, *The Blueprint2: The Gift & The Curse*. Roc-A-Fella/Def Jams, 2002.

_____. Some People Hate, *The Blueprint2: The Gift & The Curse*. Roc-A-Fella/Def Jams, 2002.

_____. Diamond Is Forever, *The Blueprint2: The Gift & The Curse*. Roc-A-Fella/Def Jams, 2002.

_____. I Did It My Way, *The Blueprint2: The Gift & The Curse*. Roc-A-Fella/Def Jams, 2002.

_____. Meet The Parents, *The Blueprint2: The Gift & The Curse*. Roc-A-Fella/Def Jams, 2002.

_____. Some How Some Way, *The Blueprint2: The Gift & The Curse*. Roc-A-Fella/Def Jams, 2002.

_____. Excuse Me Miss, *The Blueprint2: The Gift & The Curse*. Roc-A-Fella/Def Jams, 2002.

_____. All Around the World, *The Blueprint2: The Gift & The Curse*. Roc-A-Fella/Def Jams, 2002.

_____. The Watcher 2, *The Blueprint2: The Gift & The Curse*. Roc-A-Fella/Def Jams, 2002.

_____.'03 Bonnie & Clyde (feat. Beyoncé), *The Blueprint2: The Gift & The Curse*. Roc-A-Fella/Def Jams, 2002.

_____. Public Service Announcement (Interlude), *The Black Album*. Roc-A-Fella/Def Jam, 2003.

_____. December 4th, *The Black Album*. Roc-A-Fella/Def Jam, 2003.

_____. Dirt Off Your Shoulder, *The Black Album*. Roc-A-Fella/Def Jam, 2003.

_____. Encore, *The Black Album*. Roc-A-Fella/Def Jam, 2003.

_____. What More Can I Say, *The Black Album*. Roc-A-Fella/Def Jam, 2003.

_____. Justify My Thug, *The Black Album*. Roc-A-Fella/Def Jam, 2003.

_____. I Don't Wanna Be Alone Remix (feat. Shai), *The S. Carter Collection*, Mixtape hosted by Roc-A-Fella, 2003.

_____. Beach Chair, *Kingdom Come*. Roc-A-Fella/Def Jam, 2006.

_____. Hollywood, *Kingdom Come*. Roc-A-Fella/Def Jam, 2006.

_____. Trouble, *Kingdom Come*. Roc-A-Fella/Def Jam, 2006.

_____. Oh My God, *Kingdom Come*. Roc-A-Fella/Def Jam, 2006.

_____. Kingdom Come, *Kingdom Come*. Roc-A-Fella/Def Jam, 2006.

_____. American Dreamin', *American Gangster*. Roc-A-Fella/Def Jam, 2007.

_____. Say Hello, *American Gangster*. Roc-A-Fella/Def Jam, 2007.

_____. Falling, *American Gangster*. Roc-A-Fella/Def Jam, 2007.

_____. You're Welcome (feat Mary J. Blige), 2008.

T.I. Swagga Like Us (feat. Jay-Z, Kanye West, Lil Wayne, and MIA). *Paper Trail*, Grand Hustle/Atlantic Records, 2008.

Jay-Z. Thank You, *The Blueprint 3*. Roc Nation/Atlantic Records, 2009.

_____. What We Talkin' About, *The Blueprint 3*. Roc Nation/Atlantic Records, 2009.

_____. So Ambitious, *The Blueprint 3*. Roc Nation/Atlantic Records, 2009.

_____. Reminder, *The Blueprint 3*. Roc Nation/Atlantic Records, 2009.

_____. Already Home, *The Blueprint 3*. Roc Nation/Atlantic Records, 2009.

_____. Off That, *The Blueprint 3*. Roc Nation/Atlantic Records, 2009.

_____. On To The Next, *The Blueprint 3*. Roc Nation/Atlantic Records, 2009.

_____. Run This Town, *The Blueprint 3*. Roc Nation/Atlantic Records, 2009.

_____. Real As it Gets, *The Blueprint 3*. Roc Nation/Atlantic Records, 2009.

_____. Young Forever, *The Blueprint 3*. Roc Nation/Atlantic Records, 2009.

_____. History, *More Than A Game Soundtrack*. Zone 4/Interscope, 2009.

Fabolous. Money Goes, Honey Stay (feat. Jay-Z), *Loso's Way*. Desert Storm/Def Jam, 2009.

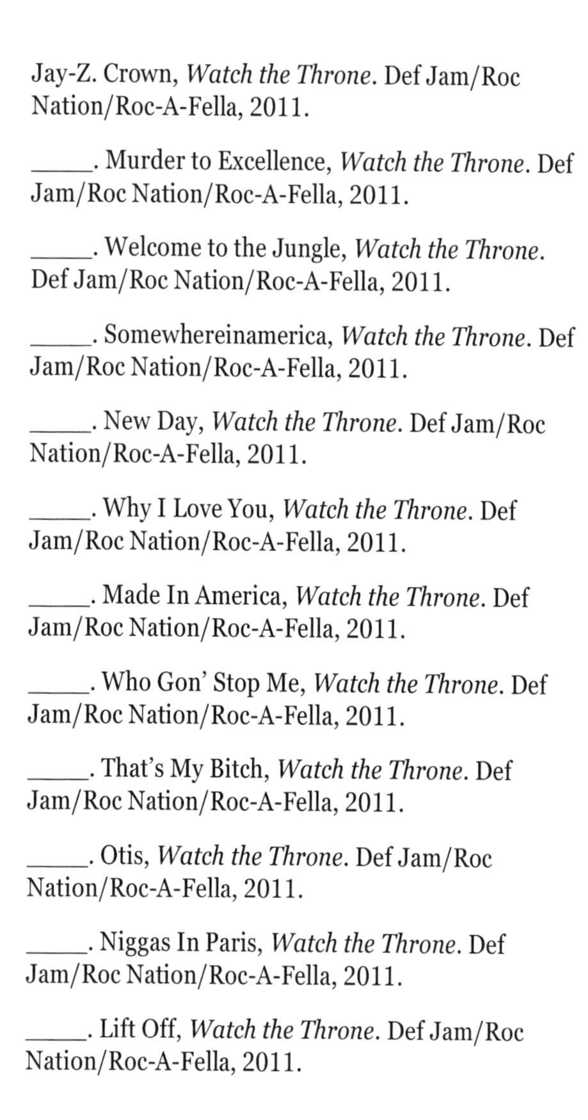
Jay-Z. Crown, *Watch the Throne*. Def Jam/Roc Nation/Roc-A-Fella, 2011.

_____. Murder to Excellence, *Watch the Throne*. Def Jam/Roc Nation/Roc-A-Fella, 2011.

_____. Welcome to the Jungle, *Watch the Throne*. Def Jam/Roc Nation/Roc-A-Fella, 2011.

_____. Somewhereinamerica, *Watch the Throne*. Def Jam/Roc Nation/Roc-A-Fella, 2011.

_____. New Day, *Watch the Throne*. Def Jam/Roc Nation/Roc-A-Fella, 2011.

_____. Why I Love You, *Watch the Throne*. Def Jam/Roc Nation/Roc-A-Fella, 2011.

_____. Made In America, *Watch the Throne*. Def Jam/Roc Nation/Roc-A-Fella, 2011.

_____. Who Gon' Stop Me, *Watch the Throne*. Def Jam/Roc Nation/Roc-A-Fella, 2011.

_____. That's My Bitch, *Watch the Throne*. Def Jam/Roc Nation/Roc-A-Fella, 2011.

_____. Otis, *Watch the Throne*. Def Jam/Roc Nation/Roc-A-Fella, 2011.

_____. Niggas In Paris, *Watch the Throne*. Def Jam/Roc Nation/Roc-A-Fella, 2011.

_____. Lift Off, *Watch the Throne*. Def Jam/Roc Nation/Roc-A-Fella, 2011.

_____. No Church in the Wild, *Watch the Throne*. Def Jam/Roc Nation/Roc-A-Fella, 2011.

_____. F.U.T.W., *Magna Carta: Holy Grail*. Roc-A-Fella/Roc Nation/ UMD, 2013.

_____. Oceans, *Magna Carta: Holy Grail*. Roc-A-Fella/Roc Nation/ UMD, 2013.

_____. Holy Grail, *Magna Carta: Holy Grail*. Roc-A-Fella/Roc Nation/ UMD, 2013.

_____. Nickels and Dimes, *Magna Carta: Holy Grail*. Roc-A-Fella/Roc Nation/ UMD, 2013.

Drake. Pound Cake/Paris Morton Music 2 (feat. Jay-Z), *Nothing Was the Same (Deluxe Edition)*. Cash Money/OVO Sounds/Young Money Entertainment, 2013.

Young Jeezy. Seen It All (Feat. JAY Z), *Seen It All: The Autobiography*. CTE/Def Jam, 2014.

Jay-Z. Bam, *4:44*. Roc Nation, 2017.

_____. Family Feud, *4:44*. Roc Nation, 2017.

_____. Kill Jay Z, *4:44*. Roc Nation, 2017.

_____. Moonlight, *4:44*. Roc Nation, 2017.

_____. Legacy, *4:44*. Roc Nation, 2017.

_____. Marcy Me, *4:44*. Roc Nation, 2017.

_____. 4:44, *4:44*. Roc Nation, 2017.

_____. Caught Their Eyes, *4:44*. Roc Nation, 2017.

_____. Smile, *4:44*. Roc Nation, 2017.

_____. The Story of O.J., *4:44*. Roc Nation, 2017.

_____. Blue's Freestyle/We Family, *4:44*. Roc Nation, 2017.

_____. ManyFacedGod, *4:44*. Roc Nation, 2017.

The Carters. 713, *EVERYTHING IS LOVE*. Parkwood/Sony/Roc Nation, 2018.

_____. FRIENDS, *EVERYTHING IS LOVE*. Parkwood/Sony/Roc Nation, 2018.

_____. BLACK EFFECT, *EVERYTHING IS LOVE*. Parkwood/Sony/Roc Nation, 2018.

_____. LOVEHAPPY, *EVERYTHING IS LOVE*. Parkwood/Sony/Roc Nation, 2018.

_____. APESH*T, *EVERYTHING IS LOVE*. Parkwood/Sony/Roc Nation, 2018.

_____. BOSS, *EVERYTHING IS LOVE*. Parkwood/Sony/Roc Nation, 2018.

_____. NICE, *EVERYTHING IS LOVE*. Parkwood/Sony/Roc Nation, 2018.

Jay-Z I Need Love, Freestyle (Live Performance), Year Unknown.

Jay-Z. B-Sides (Live Performance), May 17, 2015.

Jay-Z & Dean Baquet Interview. The New York Times Style Magazine, September 29, 2017

Johnathan Ross Show (Interview) June 27, 2008